MICHAEL E. TIGAR HAS WORKED FOR OVER FIFTY years with movements for social change as a human rights lawyer, law professor, and writer. As an attorney, Tigar argued seven cases before the U.S. Supreme Court, worked in opposition to the death penalty, and participated in international human rights cases. In 1980, with co-counsel Samuel Buffone, Tigar successfully represented the families of former Chilean Ambassador Orlando Letelier and Ronni Karpen Moffitt, who were killed by agents of Augusto Pinochet's military junta. His clients, over the years, have included H. Rap Brown (Jamil Abdullah Al-Amin), Angela Y. Davis, Leonard Peltier, and Lynne Stewart. As a professor, Tigar has taught at law schools in the United States, France, South Africa, and Japan. He is Emeritus Professor at Duke Law School and American University Washington College of Law. Tigar's literary career encompasses fifteen books, three plays, and scores of articles and essays. His book, *Law and the Rise of Capitalism*, first published by Monthly Review Press, has been translated into Spanish, Portuguese, Greek, Turkish, and Chinese. His memoir, published in 2002, is *Fighting Injustice*.

Mythologies of State and Monopoly Power

MICHAEL E. TIGAR

MONTHLY REVIEW PRESS

New York

Library of Congress Cataloging-in-Publication Data
available from the publisher.

Names: Tigar, Michael E., 1941– author.
Title: Mythologies of state and monopoly power / Michael E. Tigar.
Description: New York : Monthly Review Press, 2018.
Identifiers: LCCN 2018038348 (print) | LCCN 2018039071 (ebook) |
ISBN 9781583677445 (trade) | ISBN 9781583677452 (institutional) |
ISBN 9781583677421 (pbk.) | ISBN 9781583677438 (hardcover)
Subjects: LCSH: Law—United States. | Justice, Administration of—
United States. | Human rights—United States.
Classification: LCC KF384 (ebook) | LCC KF384 .T54 2018 (print) |
DDC 340/.1140973—dc23
LC record available at https://lccn.loc.gov/2018038348

Typeset in Minion Pro

MONTHLY REVIEW PRESS, NEW YORK
monthlyreview.org

5 4 3 2 1

Contents

Mythologies, Mental Shortcuts, Impressions

THIS BOOK IS A COLLECTION of essays. Some of them focus on how mythologies mask state repression of democratic rights in the fields of racism, criminal justice, free expression, worker rights, and international human rights. Others deal with the ways that ordinary private law categories of property, contract, and tort perform the same social function.

Mythologies are structures of words and images that portray people, institutions, and events in ways that mask an underlying reality. In the days when France used the guillotine, the executioner cried, just after the blade dropped, "*Au nom du peuple français, justice est faite.*" In the name of the French people, justice is done. This cry had no rational relation to discourse about what is fair, right, decent, or in accord with evidence about conduct. "Justice" was a name given to an event, to elevate the act of killing into an acceptable and rational process.

To proclaim "Justice" committed two solecisms. First, it appropriated justice as the exclusive property of the state. Second, it assigned a fictitious value to the word, invoking a mythology of the universality of language.

In the United States, there is a department that calls itself Justice. Colloquially, we use the term "criminal justice system," as though we are invited to ignore a system of endemic unfairness that has produced mass incarceration.

In 1957, the French writer Roland Barthes published a series of essays, under the title *Mythologies*. The book appeared in English under the same title in 1972.

Barthes's essays describe the ways in which the state, the media, and private power wielders deploy verbal and pictorial images. Barthes writes of seeing a magazine cover in the late 1950s showing a black soldier saluting the French flag. At that time, France was engaged in brutal suppression of anti-colonial uprisings in Africa and had recently lost the decisive battle of Điện Biên Phủ in Vietnam. The photograph sends the mythological message that even this soldier, and by extension most people of color, support colonialism.[1]

Another of Barthes's essays discusses the trial of a semi-literate octogenarian French goatherd for killing an English tourist. The defendant did not possess the culpable mental state that the law's machinery attributed to him. But, as Barthes observed:

> Periodically, some trial, and not necessarily fictitious like the one in Camus's *The Stranger*, comes to remind you that the Law is always prepared to lend you a spare brain in order to condemn you without remorse, and that, like Corneille, it depicts you as you should be, and not as you are.

The nineteenth-century French artist Honoré Daumier penned a cartoon of a judge facing a defendant who had stolen food. "You were hungry?" the judge declaims. "You were hungry? I myself am hungry three times a day, and I don't steal for that!"

Samuel Butler noted that parishioners in his church would be equally horrified at seeing the Christian religion doubted and at seeing it practiced.

In the United States, mythologies based on racial, ethnic, gender, and religious stereotypes drive discussions about social policy. Tom Paxton wrote of mythologies in the song "What Did You Learn in School Today?": "I learned that Washington never told a lie / I learned that soldiers seldom die . . ."

We use *mental shortcuts* to get through our daily lives. We may know how to fry an egg. The routine is semi-automatic. We don't think about every step. I need not think through all the decisions I make when crossing the street: Am I at the corner, is the WALK sign illuminated, are there cars coming, how high is the curb, and so on. I go through a series of internalized reactions, actions that "go without saying." In New York City, of course, to hell with all that, I just barge across the street like everybody else.

Some mental shortcuts are *stereotypes*. We have a bad feeling about certain people based on their race, religious practices, choice of clothes, or any of a hundred different things. If I am in lower Manhattan, near the headquarters of Goldman Sachs, and I see a well-dressed white man coming out of the building, I will cross the street to get away from him. I fear he will rob me of my pension.

Many of these stereotypes are, when viewed rationally, indefensible. Yet, when they are challenged, we are likely to hold on to them more closely. This sort of thing is sometimes called "confirmation bias." When we hold on to a position or idea in the face of contrary evidence, social science research terms this the "backfire effect."[2]

An *impression* is our "take" on something we see. Claude Monet was an "impressionist" painter. He painted the same scene, for example, the Rouen Cathedral, over and over. Each of those paintings gives us a different impression of the same scene.

All of these terms, which I often use interchangeably, refer to ways of seeing and interpreting the world around us. As I say, most of them are harmless and even useful ways of getting through the day. Some, however, are ways we fool ourselves, or permit ourselves to be fooled, about what is really going on. William James said, "A great many people think they are thinking when they are merely rearranging their prejudices."

In human rights litigation, and indeed in all law practice, we must deconstruct the myths that have grown up around our clients, the groups to which they belong, and the conduct attributed to them. Based on our client's race, social class, sexual orientation, or some other characteristic, the state rationalizes its treating our client especially harshly.

When we litigate cases, we confront not only the evidence adduced and the legal principles being argued, but also the socially, culturally, and historically determined attitudes of judges and jurors. In a jury trial, we use *voir dire* to uncover those. We look up the biographies and prior decisions of judges.

I am a human rights lawyer. My most important task is to expose, analyze, and combat the mythologies that dominate legal ideology. These mythologies form a systematic justification for the way that state power and private economic power is wielded. The essays in this book focus on how mythologies may be understood and exposed. This "myth-busting" lies at the heart of the lawyer's work. We undertake to represent clients who are marginalized. To borrow a phrase from artist and art critic John Berger, we mediate between what is given and what is desired.

The essays in this collection address five groups of mythologies that help to rationalize the present system of social relations: racism, criminal justice, free expression, worker rights, and human rights. They deconstruct what the state and the wielders of monopoly power tell us, in order to seek out what is really going on.

Throughout these essays, I repeat a theme: the law is not what it says, but what it does. What "it does" is so often based on assumptions that time and the tide of events have shown to be false. Karl Marx wrote, "The law shows its *a posteriori* to the people, as God to his servant Moses."[3] As Anatole France famously wrote: "'The majestic equality of the laws, which forbid the rich as well as the poor to sleep under bridges, to beg in the streets and to steal bread.'"

The "law" is itself an ideology, constructed to define, defend, and enforce a system of social relations. Its mythologies are enshrined as precedents. Jonathan Swift wrote in *Gulliver's Travels*:

> It is a maxim among these lawyers, that whatever hath been done before may legally be done again: and therefore they take special care to record all the decisions formerly made against common justice and the general reason of mankind. These, under the name of precedents, they produce as authorities, to justify the most iniquitous opinions; and the judges never fail of decreeing accordingly.

If we focus only on what "the law" says, we catch ourselves saying that "the law has evolved," which is like saying that "the market has crashed," or "the bank has failed," or "the car did not stop at the red light." This formulation reifies and mystifies legal rules, and if accepted leads to alienation and disempowerment. The law is not the juristic incarnation of Adam Smith's "invisible hand." People operate it. Other people can resist it and change it. And if those people are lawyers steeped in constitutional history and tradition, they have a duty to change it.

To speak of "the law" changing risks mischaracterizing mythology-busting. Several years ago, a lawyer argued in the United States Supreme Court that persons of the same sex have a constitutional right to marry. Justice Scalia asked the lawyer, when did same-sex marriage become a constitutional right? Was it 1789, or when the Fourteenth Amendment was ratified, or when? The lawyer replied that the Court had never thought such a question required answer.

To see how absurd that question was, one might ask rhetorically—as my wife did when she heard the argument and the justice's question—when did the earth begin to revolve around the sun. Was it when the Pythagoreans proposed that it did, or when Copernicus confirmed it? When did racial segregation in schools become unconstitutional? Was it not until *Brown v. Board of Education*, or had it always been at odds with the text and spirit of the Fourteenth Amendment? No, busting mythologies brings hitherto disregarded truths to bear upon outworn structures of words and thought.

Busting mythologies is not only the work of lawyers. Lawyers do it because they confront institutions of state and monopoly power in a particular way and within a determined structure. But the struggle for human liberation makes mythology-busting the business of all of us. As the Nigerian poet Wole Soyinka wrote: "The Truth shall set you free? Maybe. But first the Truth must be set free."

We will not find "Justice" uniquely in the words and work of lawyers, any more than we would find it in the basket under the guillotine. We will find it in human stories and human experience. The struggle for human liberation can be assisted and protected in some significant ways by what lawyers and their clients are able to achieve. Ultimately, people in motion will decide matters.

The essays in this book deal with claims for justice, "rights" if you will. You will find that once mythology is cast aside, the rights we value are not the product of the present system of social relations. Rather, these rights are in tension with, and in contradiction to, that system. Changing the system then becomes the next task.

Twenty-five years ago, I wrote a play titled *Haymarket: Whose Name the Few Still Say with Tears*.[4] I imagined a conversation between Clarence Darrow, who first became involved in human rights defense as he sought a pardon for the surviving defendants of the Haymarket trial,[5] and Lucy Parsons, widow of one of the Haymarket defendants who had become a leader of the anarchist movement in the early 1900s.[6] In one scene, Darrow and Parsons meet on a Chicago street:

> **DARROW:** Lucy, I'm sorry I'm late. The train from Springfield was delayed. Governor Small has pardoned the Communist Labor defendants.
> **LUCY PARSONS:** Another victory for civil liberty, Clarence. Another supplication to the state.
> **DARROW:** Another victory for the law.
> **LUCY PARSONS:** Wrong! A victory, perhaps, for the lawyers. Your lawyers' victories, Clarence, are like fireflies. You catch them and put them in a jar. By morning, their light has gone out. And your bugs are dead.

Later in the play, Parsons mocks Darrow:

Lucy Parsons: Your lawyer's ego wants you to think you stand at the center of every event by which the world is changed. Your right to stand there is only because some brave soul has risked death or prison in the people's cause and you are called to defend him—or her. When you put law and lawyers at the center of things, you are only getting in the people's way, and doing proxy for the image of the law the state wants us to have. The law is a mask that the state puts on when it wants to commit some indecency upon the oppressed.

Darrow: (*angry*) If I believed that, I would still be **a** lawyer for the railroad, and not making do with the fees the union can pay. Lucy, the law is a fence built around the people and their rights.

Lucy Parsons: (*kindly*) What an image! And you, Clarence, are a fierce old dog, set to bark and warn off intruders.

In that imagined debate between Darrow and Parsons, they are both right. Many of the essays in this book discuss victories won in courts by lawyers on behalf of clients. To imagine that those victories have wrought—or could have wrought—fundamental and lasting social change would be to embrace a disabling and disempowering mythology. We lawyers try cases. We provide outcomes, not solutions.

Lawyers who exaggerate the importance of their professional training may be forgiven. Too much of legal education these days is focused on cases and principles, and does not descend (or ascend, I think) to the study of the human conditions that are at the root of the matter. Most law students have never personally experienced or shared the injustices that their potential clients have faced. They are taught the principles of law and legal analysis. Clinical legal education programs, now a feature of most law school curricula, can play an important role by introducing students to what law "does" as distinct from what it "says."

Let me try out a metaphor. On the walls of a beautiful ancient Zen temple in Japan are paintings of tigers. I like paintings of tigers. But these tigers do not look like any tiger you or I have ever seen. They are more like house cats done bigger and with stripes, and their expressions are not at all tiger-like.

The reason is that these painters had never seen a tiger. They had read reports from those who had seen tigers. And so it is with those who paint pictures of legal rules that are claimed to be good and proper, but who have never seen or studied or mingled with the people to whom these rules are to be applied. Anyone, including a lawyer, who wants to play a role in the struggle for human liberation had best begin by finding out what is really going on.

In 2014, the cases about the right to marry were pending in courts across the nation. In one such case, the Court of Appeals denied that right, by a vote of 2 to 1. The majority opinion was an excursus into generalities of social policy and the supposed limits of judicial power to address fundamental questions. This is a form of judicial detachment that we will see again in this book. The dissenting judge, Martha Daughtrey, exposed the mythology inherent in the majority opinion:

> The author of the majority opinion has drafted what would make an engrossing TED Talk or, possibly, an introductory lecture in Political Philosophy. But as an appellate court decision, it wholly fails to grapple with the relevant constitutional question in this

appeal: whether a state's constitutional prohibition of same-sex marriage violates equal protection under the Fourteenth Amendment. Instead, the majority sets up a false premise—that the question before us is "who should decide?"—and leads us through a largely irrelevant discourse on democracy and federalism. In point of fact, the real issue before us concerns what is at stake in these six cases for the individual plaintiffs and their children, and what should be done about it. . . .

In the main, the majority treats both the issues and the litigants here as mere abstractions. Instead of recognizing the plaintiffs as persons, suffering actual harm as a result of being denied the right to marry where they reside or the right to have their valid marriages recognized there, my colleagues view the plaintiffs as social activists who have somehow stumbled into federal court, inadvisably, when they should be out campaigning to win "the hearts and minds" of Michigan, Ohio, Kentucky, and Tennessee voters to their cause. But these plaintiffs are not political zealots trying to push reform on their fellow citizens; they are committed same-sex couples, many of them heading up de facto families, who want to achieve equal status—de jure status, if you will—with their married neighbors, friends, and coworkers, to be accepted as contributing members of their social and religious communities, and to be welcomed as fully legitimate parents at their children's schools. They seek to do this by virtue of exercising a civil right that most of us take for granted—the right to marry. Readers who are familiar with the . . . Seventh Circuit's opinion in *Baskin v. Bogan*, 766 F.3d 648, 654 (7th Cir. 2014) ("Formally these cases are about discrimination against the small homosexual minority in the United States. But at a deeper level . . . they are about the welfare of American children."), must have said to themselves at various points in the majority opinion, "But what about the children?"

In 2015, the Supreme Court upheld Judge Daughtrey's position.[7]

Mythologies of Racism

FEAR, LOATHING, AND MYTH I: THE JAPANESE INTERNMENT AND MANIPULATED FEAR

IN THE UNITED STATES LEGAL system, mythologies based on race have been persistent and endemic. In early 1942, under an executive order signed by President Roosevelt, more than 120,000 Japanese Americans in the western part of the United States were rounded up and placed in prison camps.[8] Almost two-thirds of those imprisoned were American citizens. The justification for this action was that some Japanese Americans might possibly help the Japanese war effort by such things as signaling submarines. In *Korematsu v. United States*, the six Supreme Court justices who voted to uphold the internment justified this mass incarceration as a wartime measure, adding:

> The judgment that exclusion of the whole group was, for the same reason, a military imperative answers the contention that the exclusion was in the nature of group punishment based on antagonism to those of Japanese origin.

Justice Frank Murphy, in dissent, called it what it was:

This exclusion of "all persons of Japanese ancestry, both alien and non-alien," from the Pacific Coast area on a plea of military necessity in the absence of martial law ought not to be approved. Such exclusion goes over "the very brink of constitutional power," and falls into the ugly abyss of racism.

Justice Jackson, who was later to be a prosecutor at the Nuremberg trials, noted:

Korematsu was born on our soil, of parents born in Japan. The Constitution makes him a citizen of the United States by nativity, and a citizen of California by residence. No claim is made that he is not loyal to this country. There is no suggestion that he is not law-abiding and well disposed.

How could six smart, well-educated people subscribe to the mythologies that motivated the internment? They had seen the Nazi rise to power. Indeed, the majority opinion testily rejects a claim that the internment centers were "concentration camps." Their law library—and some of their earlier decisions—contained many eloquent testaments to the way that racism and xenophobia can mislead decision-makers.

Mythologies are resilient. They do not easily yield to arguments based on generalities about fairness, tolerance, and justice. We advocates for victims of mythological thinking about racism, sexism, xenophobia, and political repression can do our job only if we truly, deeply see our clients and their concerns as they really are and not as we imagine them to be or, worse yet, as the state would have us see them. We insist that what the law "does" or is about to do must be justified by lawful, logical, relevant evidence, and that legal standards be precise and intelligible.

Once we see our clients as they are, we must confront and challenge the false picture that the state wants to paint. This can be a challenge because those who uphold the mythology have no compunction about hiding the truth. In the internment cases, Solicitor General Fahy, representing the government, suppressed two important pieces of evidence: one was an official intelligence report showing that mass internment was not necessary and that legitimate goals could be achieved by individually considering cases of alleged disloyalty. The other was a document casting doubt on claims that Japanese-Americans had aided the Japanese war effort. Based on racial stereotypes and false evidence, six justices accepted the idea that sinister motives lurked in the minds and hearts of countless Japanese Americans, and that the road from those hidden motives to wholesale sabotage was short and swift.

The mythologies that justify a leap from perceived danger to repression are with us always. We recall Auden's words: "I smell blood and an era of prominent madmen."

Here is a story that John Henry Faulk told. John Henry was a comic genius, a populist philosopher, and a worthy citizen. He had survived the blacklist.[9] One evening in Austin, Texas, in the 1980s, he was on the dais with the director of the FBI. The director spoke of the great social dangers against which the power of government was protecting us. John Henry stood and (as I recall it) said:

> Well, that was a fine speech. A lot of people don't know that I myself was in law enforcement. I was a United States Marshal. I was ten years old. My territory was

along the banks of Lake Austin, and I patrolled it with my deputy, Johnny Wilson. Now as it happens, the Faulk henhouse was in our territory, and we regularly patrolled it. One day, we went into the henhouse. There were no eggs in the nest boxes. So we thought maybe the hens had got up on the high shelf to lay. Johnny got up on tiptoe and ran his hand up on that shelf. And wouldn't you know it, there was a chicken snake up there. Johnny screamed "Chicken snake!" and we turned to run. But the henhouse door had swung shut and latched, so we broke it down and escaped into the yard. The noise brought my mother running. "What are you boys doing?" "Mrs. Faulk," Johnny cried, "there's a chicken snake in there!" "Well, Johnny, don't you know that a chicken snake can't hurt you?" "Yes, ma'am," Johnny said, "but it can scare you so much you'll hurt yourself!"

FEAR, LOATHING, AND MYTH II: "SEPARATE BUT EQUAL" AND THE LAND WHERE SUPREME COURT JUSTICES DWELL

I have been reading with pleasure the work of Paul Beatty, whose novel *The Sellout* won the Man Booker Prize for 2016. *The Sellout*, and his earlier novel, *The White Boy Shuffle*, illuminate many mythologies about race. His anthology of humor, *Hokum*, is also a gem. I also like Charles Mackay's 1841 book, *Extraordinary Popular Delusions and the Madness of Crowds*. Though the book deals with "popular" and not "governmental" delusions, it describes historic events that may serve as a warning for these times. The book's epigraph speaks broadly of "delusions of the human spirit" (*délires de l'esprit humain*).

The Sellout deals with racial segregation in the schools, from Beatty's challenging perspective. After reading it, I was impelled to revisit the course of judicial decision that led to *Brown v. Board of Education* in 1954.

Most people know about *Plessy v. Ferguson.*[10] Homer Plessy bought a train ticket in Louisiana and took a seat in the "whites-only" car. He refused to move to the "colored" car. He was arrested and charged with violating a Louisiana statute, the Separate Car Act, which mandated racial segregation on railroads. The Supreme Court held, over Justice Harlan's dissent, that racial separation was permissible in public accommodations, assuming that the accommodations for each race were substantially equal. Justice Brown, for the majority, wrote:

> Laws permitting, and even requiring, their separation, in places where they are liable to be brought into contact, do not necessarily imply the inferiority of either race to the other, and have been generally, if not universally, recognized as within the competency of the state legislatures in the exercise of their police power.

And this:

> If one race be inferior to the other socially, the Constitution of the United States cannot put them upon the same plane. . . . We consider the underlying fallacy of the plaintiff's argument to consist in the assumption that the enforced separation of the two races stamps the colored race with a badge of inferiority. If this be so, it is not by reason of anything found in the act, but solely because the colored race chooses to put that construction upon it.

Thus, seven justices, each of whom had to know that since

1872 Southern states had enacted a comprehensive system of Jim Crow laws as a means of denying African Americans equal treatment, declared the African Americans' sense that this might be invidious discrimination to be a myth that "the colored race" might unwisely indulge. These justices also knew or should have known of the KKK, lynchings, and all the other phenomena of white rule.

To justify these views, the Court cited cases upholding racial segregation in schools, public accommodation, and transportation. No matter that many of these cases described practices that antedated the Civil War. By the time *Plessy* was decided, the Court had already trivialized the Fourteenth Amendment and in so doing ignored the lesson that the War Between the States ought to have taught.[11] As Paul Beatty has suggested, some folks think "antebellum" is a cranky old white lady.

The mythology of separate equality, set out in *Plessy*, persisted. In 1941, in *Railroad Commission of Texas v. Pullman Co.*,[12] the Supreme Court refused to confront it. The Texas Railroad Commission enacted a regulation providing that sleeping cars on trains running through Texas, and therefore indisputably operating in interstate commerce, must have a conductor in charge of the sleeping cars and not a porter. All train conductors where white, and almost all sleeping car porters were African-American. The railroad, the Pullman Company, and the Brotherhood of Sleeping Car Porters sued, alleging that the regulation violated the Fourteenth Amendment equal protection clause.

Note the alliance of plaintiffs here, where the notoriously anti-union Pullman Company and the at least mildly anti-union railroad joined an African American labor organization in bringing the lawsuit. We see the same kinds of alliances in, for example, challenges to gender discrimination:

corporate employers know that recruitment and retention of qualified workers is harmed when the state permits or mandates discrimination based on sexual orientation, gender, race, or ethnicity.

The lawsuit did not require reexamination of "separate but equal." Here was a state law that, based on race, forbade private employers to choose employees who would perform certain functions.

Shamefully, the unanimous Supreme Court ducked the issue. Its rationale survives as something called "*Pullman* abstention," and many if not most books that discuss it do not pause to remark just how tawdry was the reasoning that gave rise to this principle. Justice Frankfurter justified the Court's refusal to decide:

> The complaint of the Pullman porters undoubtedly tendered a substantial constitutional issue. It is more than substantial. It touches a sensitive area of social policy upon which the federal courts ought not to enter unless no alternative to its adjudication is open.

Thus, white Texas bureaucrats were allowed to override not only the Fourteenth Amendment equal protection clause but also the judgment of the Pullman Company and the railroad, two entities that would be most aware of the social and economic consequences of having porters staff the sleeping cars.

The mythology here was that the Supreme Court's assertedly delicate role as constitutional arbiter must be played cautiously, deferentially, and remote from grim realities such as racism. In shirking its constitutional responsibility, the Court also turned its back on earlier decisions that, in the process of upholding racial discrimination, had invalidated state laws that overrode private transportation companies' decisions to discriminate. Yes, the Court had already been down this road. Only when the path beckoned toward recognizing the constitutional right did it call a halt.

The candid admission that the Court was backing away from its duty is even more surprising because Justice Frankfurter wrote the opinion. He had, as a Harvard professor, co-authored a scathing study of ethnic discrimination and injustice in the Sacco and Vanzetti case.[13] In a later decision, *West Virginia State Board of Education v. Barnette*,[14] he began his dissenting opinion by saying that he "belongs to the most vilified and persecuted minority in history." In *Watts v. Indiana*,[15] he wrote: "There comes a point where this Court should not be ignorant as judges of what we know as men." Among the things he knew as a man was that he worked in one of the most racially segregated cities in the United States.

Here is some of the background against which the *Pullman* case was decided—or not decided. In 1869, the Reconstruction legislature of Louisiana passed a statute forbidding racial discrimination in transportation within the state. The case arose because a steamboat company plying the Mississippi River had separate accommodations for white and African American passengers. The statute applied even to the intrastate portion of interstate journeys.

In *Hall v. DeCuir*,[16] the Supreme Court held the statute unconstitutional because it interfered with the business of federally regulated interstate transportation. The Court noted that Congress had not seen fit to forbid racial segregation, and therefore the transportation companies were free to discriminate if they wished to do so. The Court held:

1. State legislation that interferes with an interstate carrier's conduct of its own business violates the commerce

clause. (Note that in *Pullman*, that is exactly what Texas was doing.)

2. The transportation company is constitutionally protected when it adopts "reasonable rules and regulations," including those based on race. This holding was based on deference to the transportation company's judgment about the social consequences of white and non-white passengers sharing cabins on board.

In *Pullman*, the Court could have cited *Hall*, and said that Texas had to stand down. But it chose instead to first see the real issue—racism—and then to refuse to address it.

THE LAST GASP OF "SEPARATE BUT EQUAL"

In *Sweatt v. Painter*,[17] the Supreme Court held, unanimously, that a makeshift "Texas Law School for Negroes" did not provide equal, though separate, legal education.

Heman Sweatt applied to enter the University of Texas School of Law in 1946. He was denied admission because the Texas state constitution mandated segregated public education. No law school in Texas admitted African Americans. The NAACP, whose lawyers included Robert Carter and Thurgood Marshall, sued in state court. At the state's request, the court continued the case for six months. The state then established the "School of Law of the Texas State University for Negroes" and claimed that it was substantially equal to the UT Law School.

By the time the case reached the Supreme Court, in 1950, the civil rights movement had been active for decades. The NAACP was founded in 1909; the struggle against racism had begun earlier than that. More recently, President Truman had desegregated the armed forces. The state's Supreme

Court brief[18] was written as though none of these things had happened. It was as though written on the inside walls of the lawyers' minds. It was a voluntary petition in intellectual bankruptcy, repeating the mythology of racial separation. The brief relied on cases denying equal protection to aliens, and approvingly cited the Japanese internment cases. Concluding, the state argued:

> The foregoing cases argue themselves. They demonstrate that this Court has uniformly held that the states may furnish education to their white and Negro citizens at separate institutions so long as substantially equal facilities are offered both groups. Petitioner has cited no case to the contrary.

The state assembled a litany of opinions about segregation. Sweatt's lawyers had combed the sociological and political literature of the past decade. Their 123-page brief[19] adumbrated the ideas that were to be presented and would carry the day in *Brown v. Board of Education*.

The state's brief quoted Charles W. Eliot, who was president of Harvard College from 1869 to 1909. Eliot had spoken approvingly of segregated higher education in the American South:

> Perhaps if there were as many Negroes here as there, we might think it better for them to be in separate schools. At present Harvard has about 5,000 white students and about 30 of the colored race. The latter are hidden in the great mass and are not noticeable. If they were equal in numbers or in a majority, we might deem a separation necessary.

Sort of like rice pudding, I suppose. A few raisins do not dominate, nor destroy the essential white rice character of the pudding. Too many raisins, and there is a risk that they will take over. Better they should be removed into a raisin pudding. You might leave a few raisins, to serve the white rice and remind it of its dominance.

The state should have done what good lawyers do: check out their witness. On several subjects, Eliot was out of step with all reasoned opinion.[20] He opposed having a college football team and tried to abolish football, baseball, basketball, and hockey at Harvard. Rowing and tennis were, he thought, clean sports. As for baseball, Eliot remarked:

> Well, this year I'm told the team did well because one pitcher had a fine curve ball. I understand that a curve ball is thrown with a deliberate attempt to deceive. Surely this is not an ability we should want to foster at Harvard.

Eliot spoke about race in Atlanta in 1909. The *New York Times* reported his views at the time: "The negro cannot be expected to be ready for all phases of civilization, when he is a few decades removed from the time when he first began to enjoy civilization as a free man. After 500 or 1,000 years we may expect more substantial growth." Dr. Eliot had forgotten that the "civilization" that African Americans had joined was the very one that had maintained the very uncivilized institution of slavery.

Turning to the evidence at trial, the state quoted the testimony of Charles T. McCormick. He was dean of UT Law School from 1940 to 1949, and was nominally dean of the segregated law school. The Law School for Negroes had four professors, who were faculty members of UT Law School and who taught part-time at the segregated school. It had a couple of classrooms and a small library in downtown Austin. As Sweatt's brief pointed out:

> The law school of the University of Texas had a moot court, legal aid clinic, law review, a chapter of Order of the Coif, and a scholarship fund. None of these were present or possible in the proposed Negro law school, and Charles T. McCormick, dean of the two law schools, testified that he did not consider these to be factors material to a legal education but rather that they were "extraneous matters."

McCormick's views were echoed by D. A. Simmons, a prominent Texas lawyer who had been chairman of the American Judicature Society and president of the American Bar Association. The Supreme Court's unanimous opinion penetrated the myth:

> Moreover, although the law is a highly learned profession, we are well aware that it is an intensely practical one. The law school, the proving ground for legal learning and practice, cannot be effective in isolation from the individuals and institutions with which the law interacts. Few students and no one who has practiced law would choose to study in an academic vacuum, removed from the interplay of ideas and the exchange of views with which the law is concerned. The law school to which Texas is willing to admit petitioner excludes from its student body members of the racial groups which number 85% of the population of the State and include most

of the lawyers, witnesses, jurors, judges and other officials with whom petitioner will inevitably be dealing when he becomes a member of the Texas Bar. With such a substantial and significant segment of society excluded, we cannot conclude that the education offered petitioner is substantially equal to that which he would receive if admitted to the University of Texas Law School.

The Court ordered Mr. Sweatt admitted to the University of Texas Law School.

Looking back at the history and record of the *Sweatt* case, one is struck by how transparent were some of the justifications offered to keep Mr. Sweatt out of the University of Texas Law School. Charles T. McCormick could not possibly have believed that a law review, Order of the Coif, and moot court were extraneous to modern legal education. McCormick was one of the most eminent United States experts on the law of *evidence*, that is, the rules by which matters are decided using rational, probative proof.

THE PERSISTENCE OF RACIST MYTHOLOGIES

The myths on which segregation was based had, by 1950, become transparent, but not to everyone. School districts responded to the 1954 decision in *Brown v. Board of Education* by refusing to desegregate unless and until a drawn-out lawsuit resulted in a final judgment requiring them to do so. So there was litigation in hundreds of school districts. The *Brown* decision, and Chief Justice Warren, were denounced, even in the pages of the *American Bar Association Journal*. In a 1956 *Journal* article, two prominent lawyers decried "the commingling of the white and colored races" and the effect this might have on "white children and their parents."[21]

Thus, when the mythology of "separate but equal" was exposed, the political and social forces that supported racism did not run up a white (what other color could it be?) flag of surrender. Other mythological constructs were brought into play. The American South's myth of a gracious past overlay the reality of its brutal present.

Mythologies can be exposed in courtrooms, where a more or less orderly procedure allows reliable evidence to be heard and nonsense rejected. Such proceedings help us understand the world. The point, however—as somebody said—is to change it.

Racist mythologies appear in different guises. They are shape-shifters. We can spot them by their results and by examining the motivations of those who put them forward. Some expressions are obvious. In 2014, a fourth-grade teacher at a private school in Wisconsin gave her students a homework assignment: "Give 3 'good' reasons for slavery and 3 bad reasons. Make notes and then put them into COMPLETE SENTENCES on a separate sheet to prepare for presenting an argument."[22]

Of late, racist mythologies are called out with coded words that have acquired the name "dog whistles." Here are some examples:

- **"PRIVATE PROPERTY"**: Impatient with the pace of change, students in Greensboro, North Carolina. held a lunch counter sit-in on February 1, 1960. From this beginning, a direct-action movement spread across the nation. The owners of restaurants, lunch counters, hotels, trains, and buses invoked property rights.
- **"FREE ASSOCIATION"**: Employers mobilized white em-

ployees with slogans claiming that African-American workers would steal their jobs. Racist rhetoric was used to resist campaigns for union organization. Entrenched leadership in the craft unions sought to exclude African Americans from union membership.

- **"Mississippi Freedom Summer":** Freedom Summer 1964 was a dramatic chapter in the movement for civil rights. Thousands of civil rights adherents came to Mississippi to work on the denial of voting rights and other institutional forms of racism. Racists fought back. The toll included three murdered civil rights workers, many more workers injured, 250 arrests, thirteen black churches burned to the ground, two dozen other church buildings bombed or burned. At the Democratic National Convention, the struggle played out between the Mississippi Freedom Democratic Party and the "regular," segregationist Mississippi Democratic Party. On national television, we witnessed white liberals failing to meet the challenge of busting the mythology that the "regular" Mississippi Democrats could possibly "represent" Mississippi.

- **"Neighborhood Schools":** Faced with a Constitution-based ruling that segregation was unlawful, the white power structure, in the North and South of the United States, adopted a policy that students should attend the schools closest to their homes—neighborhood schools. This slogan was itself a mythological cover for racism. Residential housing was segregated, and not simply as the result of income disparity and personal choice. Richard Rothstein's brilliant book, *The Color of Law: A Forgotten History of How Our Government Segregated America*, documents how local, state, and national government policies enforced and reinforced housing segregation, with the active connivance of lending institutions.

When the mythology of neighborhood schools was challenged, the power structure decried the use of busing to create integrated schools.

- **"Racism Is Over":** Reactionary judges and politicians proclaim that the days of racism are over, and that taking race into account is a form of invidious discrimination—against whites. Fortunately, other judges express a view that reflects the history and text of the Thirteenth, Fourteenth, and Fifteenth amendments. Rejecting a challenge to affirmative action at the University of Texas, the Supreme Court majority, in an opinion by Justice Anthony Kennedy, returned to the principles the Court has expressed in *Sweatt v. Painter*:

  A university is in large part defined by those intangible "qualities which are incapable of objective measurement but which make for greatness." [Quoting Sweatt.] Considerable deference is owed to a university in defining those intangible characteristics, like student body diversity, that are central to its identity and educational mission. But still, it remains an enduring challenge to our Nation's education system to reconcile the pursuit of diversity with the constitutional promise of equal treatment and dignity.

- **"Stand Your Ground":** In the common law of England, which was largely imported into the United States in the 1700s, a person faced with potential deadly force had a duty to retreat if possible and avoid a confrontation.[23] Within the last two decades, almost every American state has enacted one version or another of a "stand your ground" rule, by which use of deadly force is justified whenever a person honestly apprehends fatal danger. The ostensibly neutral rule of the law is therefore that killing another human being is justified based on a rational perception of danger. In practice, "stand your ground" has been disproportionately invoked to justify white violence against people of color.

- **"To Protect and Serve":** By now, the mythology of a police presence that, without racial bias, serves and protects all persons has been exposed. In 2017, in the United States, nearly 1,000 people were shot and killed by police officers. More than 50 percent of those killed were non-white. CNN reported in 2016 that black men are three times more likely to die from police shootings than are white men. Yet prosecutions of police officers are relatively rare, because prosecutors offer up ostensibly race-neutral excuses for police conduct. In 2014, NBC reported that being killed by a police officer was the second most prevalent form of homicide in Utah during the previous five years. The police killings were, again, disproportionately of persons of color.

- **"We Are Honoring History":** Statues of Confederate leaders are in public spaces throughout the American South. A huge bas-relief carving of Robert E. Lee, Stonewall Jackson, and Jefferson Davis, at Stone Mountain Park in Georgia, is one of the most famous of these.[24] Most of the Confederate monuments have a decisively ugly history. They were not erected when memories of the Civil War were fresh. They were put up as part of the white supremacist populist wave of the early twentieth century. Many of them were erected with the support of the Ku Klux Klan. Stone Mountain's connection to the Klan is particularly odious and extensive; it was the site of many significant Klan rallies in the years since the memorial was carved. The movement to take down the so-called

Civil War statues is not designed to erase history but to reclaim and demythologize it.

2

Mythologies of Criminal Justice

PALLADIUMS AND CITADELS

THERE HAPPENS, UPON OCCASION, a judicial utterance so arresting as to require study and contemplation for what it tells us of the world in which judges dwell. [25] One such utterance is Justice Black's summing up for the majority in *Illinois v. Allen*,[26] holding that a trial judge confronted with an obstreperous defendant might hold the man in contempt, bind and gag him, or exclude him from his trial. Such a holding is necessary, the justice said, to show that "our courts, palladiums of liberty as they are, cannot be treated disrespectfully," and so that they will "remain . . . citadels of justice."

As I wonder how Justice Black could have penned that paean with a straight face, I am reminded of my first appearance in the New York criminal courts at 100 Centre Street in Manhattan. In a desperate attempt to preserve the image of justice, someone had put a big plastic bag over the American flag on the judge's dais. The bag was yellowed and grimy. Behind the judge, an incomplete set of tarnished metal letters proclaimed: IN GOD WE RUST.

I went back to 100 Centre Street in 2018. The walls have been painted and missing aluminum letters restored. The rest of it is pretty much the same.

. "In the halls of justice," Lenny Bruce used to say, "the only justice is in the halls." Maybe not in the halls, either, for that is where the plea bargains and lawyer-client conversations take place.

Learned Hand served as a federal judge in New York for more than forty years. His view of palladium and citadel was not so sanguine: "I must say that, as a litigant, I should dread a lawsuit beyond almost anything short of sickness and death."

No, for the men and women caught up in them, the criminal courts are neither palladiums of liberty nor citadels of justice. Citadels, perhaps, in the sense used by an English author in 1598: "a citadell, castell, or spacious fort built not onely to defend the citie, but also to keepe the same in awe and subiection." Unfortunately, the constitutional revolution in criminal procedure has amounted to little more than an ornament, or golden cupola, built upon the roof of a structure found rotting and infested, assuring the gentlefolk who only pass by without entering that all is well inside.

MASS INCARCERATION AND SOCIAL CONTROL

Assume that Canada and the Western European countries have about the right number of people in jail. Assume that the social problem of crime in those countries is not terribly different from that in the United States. Understand that the United States incarceration rate is five to seven times that of those other countries. If these assumptions, and this understanding, are even nearly valid, 80 percent of the people in American jails should not be there. This is mass incarceration.

The heavy toll of jailed people reflects the extent to which the criminal process is used as a mechanism of social control, directed mainly at the poor and at people of color. Thirteen percent of the U.S. population is African-American; 64 percent of those incarcerated are African-American. Sixteen percent of the population is Hispanic; Hispanics are 19 percent of the incarcerated. Until the Supreme Court began to address the issue in 2012, the United States had more than 2,500 people serving life without parole for offenses committed before they were eighteen. That was global first place; Israel came in second, with seven. This is not to mention that the United States remains one of the few countries of the world that still has the death penalty.[27]

These figures portray what I term the substantive aspect of the issue, which could also be called over-criminalization. Minor social deviance makes you subject to criminal punishment, and for prison terms that are far longer than those imposed in other countries.

Perhaps more significantly, police and prosecutorial discretion is exercised in racially discriminatory ways. A study that became the basis for a Supreme Court case, *McCleskey v. Kemp*,[28] found that prosecutors were 4.3 times more likely to seek the death penalty when a black person was accused of killing a white person than when a white person was accused of killing a black person. The Supreme Court's decision refusing to take the study into account in assessing the constitutionality of the death penalty has been condemned as one of the worst in U.S. history. Professor Anthony Amsterdam called the case "the Dred Scott decision of our time." [29]

How could such a system persist without being attacked and torn down as an obvious instrument of racism and repression? The proceduralist would tell us that these figures are not reason for alarm, for every person faced with incarceration has a mythic array of due process rights. I sat at dinner with a Supreme Court Justice, who explained to me that the Constitution was drafted by people who had read Isaac Newton, and who devised a mechanism of checks and balances, like clockwork. The Framers, he said, were concerned with the mechanism of government. This view is, to be sure, partial: the Framers had been revolutionaries, battlers for a certain social vision, threatened with jail or execution themselves. They were also white males who owned property, and many if not most of them counted human beings among their property. The clockwork idea is, however, powerful, for it reveals something of current Supreme Court attitudes toward the criminal process that puts all these people behind bars.

Clockwork is a powerful image because a clock is quintessentially "form." The substance is what time it is. If there is only one clock, and it is kept by a small group of the powerful, then the time is whatever they say it is. The clock, and even the rather arbitrary decision to divide its units into 60, 60 and 12 or 24, is itself a convention established by somebody or other.

The system of mass incarceration is shielded from just criticism by two mythologies: the mythology of fair trial and the mythology of free plea bargain.

THE MYTHOLOGY OF FAIR TRIAL

Legal counsel is at the center of the formalistic bargains that dominate the criminal process.[30] The Constitution is explicit: "No person shall be held to answer except," "the accused shall enjoy," and similar phrases introduce enumerated rights of a person charged with or suspected of a crime. Among these rights is "assistance of counsel." We must therefore define the multiple bargains by which this promise of counsel is fulfilled.

The first such bargain is the one spelled out in the Bill of Rights. Like all the other enumerated rights, the Constitution is a promise by an ostensibly neutral state, as a condition of the overall deal struck by "We the People" who established the government to begin with. This newly formed union of states, dominated by owners of property including slaves, guarantees certain rights, the scope of which it will interpret. Whether this bargain means anything depends, here as in all its other aspects, on who is wielding the levers of state power.

A Columbia Law School study found fundamental legal error in two-thirds of the capital cases tried in the United States since 1978. Most of those errors involved police officials hiding exculpatory evidence, prosecutors and police denying the accused basic rights in the criminal justice system, and judges who overlooked those errors. Many of these judges, particularly in the "Death Belt" states of the American South, are elected in campaigns designed to fire up the vengeful spirit of the majority community. Capital cases are not unique in being corrupted by error; it is only that they have been studied most closely.

This brings us to the lawyers. Regardless of how biased the judge, how inhumane the criminal law, and how corrupt and malign the police and prosecutors, the accused is supposed to have a champion, a lawyer. The *National Law Journal* did a study of appointed counsel in capital cases in 1990. Given what is at stake, one would expect that only the most qualified lawyers would be found adequate to the task. By now, almost everyone has read the anecdotal evidence that this is not so. The classic story of the Texas-appointed lawyer who slept during his client's capital murder trial has made the rounds. The trial and penalty phase lasted just thirteen hours, and the lawyer did not even make objection when the prosecutor said the jurors should sentence the defendant to death because he is gay.[31]

The *National Law Journal* found that:

- the trial lawyers who represented death row inmates in the six states were disbarred, suspended, or otherwise disciplined at a rate three to forty-six times the discipline rates for lawyers in those states.
- there were wholly unrealistic statutory fee limits on defense representation.
- there were nonexistent standards for appointment of counsel.
- capital trials were completed in one to two days, in contrast to two-week or two-month long trials in some states where indigent defense systems were operating.

In short, the right to effective counsel is ignored in the cases where the stakes are highest and error rates demonstrably high.[32] The idea that a capital case can be well tried in one or two days is laughable. In the Oklahoma City bombing trial of Terry Nichols, jury selection alone took five weeks in order to get a panel that was willing to swear it could overcome the media barrage. The trial itself took nearly three months. The defense called more than a hundred witnesses. The jury acquitted Nichols of murder, finding him guilty of lesser charges, and voted not to impose a death penalty.

In non-capital cases, the counsel situation is every bit as bleak. In April 2001 the *New York Times* published the results of its investigation into the New York City–appointed counsel system. It found that appointed counsel are paid at rates that actively discourage them from spending enough time on cases. The only way to make the appointed practice pay is by taking on hundreds of cases per year and spending as little time as possible on each one. The *Times* "poster lawyer" was one Sean Sullivan. He handled 1,600 cases per year and earned more than $125,000 in 2000 for his efforts. The "representation" he provides was worse than minimal. He did not confer with clients, did not return client phone calls, did not prepare needed legal motions, and contented himself with working out quick plea bargains on an assembly-line basis.

More recent data appears in a *New York Times* article about the excessive caseloads in the Missouri public defender system.[33] A defender assigned to a felony prosecution has only nine hours to work on the case, compared with the forty-seven hours that the study finds is necessary to do an adequate job. Many juveniles are sent off to incarceration with no lawyer at all.[34]

A 2010 study of cases in which the defendant was exonerated after being convicted and being sent to prison found that defense counsel was constitutionally ineffective in 21 percent of the cases. Deficiencies in performance ranged from failure to seek available exculpatory evidence to being drunk at trial, to sleeping through the trial.[35]

The case of *Texas v. Cobb*[36] illustrates the Supreme Court's attitude toward the role of counsel. The Court held 5 to 4 that when an indigent has counsel appointed to represent him for one crime, that representation bargain does not extend to other related offenses. Therefore the state can treat the accused as being without counsel for any offense beyond that with which he is formally charged. Suppose, for example, that an indigent is found with an unlicensed weapon, and arrested on that charge. Counsel is appointed, and the accused is held in jail. The police suspect that this defendant might have committed another crime, such as using the weapon in a robbery. Even though the accused has counsel, and even though the lawyer has told the police that counsel should be present during questioning, and even though the police have agreed to that condition, the Supreme Court's decision means that the accused may be questioned without counsel being present. The Court's reasoning is that the contract of representation, as defined by and in the interest of the state, does not extend to protecting the accused's liberty generally, but rather only to defending the specific charge.

In sharp contrast, a defendant with means to hire a private attorney will benefit from a true bargain, and not a fake one grudgingly given by the state. That defendant's lawyer will be considered by the rules of legal ethics to be counsel for all related matters.

In many if not most communities, defendants awaiting trial—and presumed innocent—may be held without bail for weeks at a time due to crowded court dockets. Because a poor person cannot post cash bond, he or she stays in jail. The racial disparity in arrest patterns is then compounded by the disparity between rich and poor. In these communities, it is often the practice not to appoint counsel until the defendant appears in court after the long delay. The social consequences of this system are that the jailed accused, though presumed innocent, loses whatever employment he or she may have had and risks a breakdown in family and community ties.[37]

True, the Constitution formally guarantees effective assistance of counsel. This ought to be, and could be if properly interpreted, a mechanism for ensuring that the "bargain" between counsel and accused reflects the client's desires and interests. Not so. Appointed counsel's duty to provide effective assistance is, in practice, governed by loose and discretionary standards. In reviewing a case to determine whether counsel was ineffective, the courts give wide latitude to so-called tactical decisions, including decisions not to investigate possible defenses, to refrain from cross-examining witnesses, and to make only token arguments to the jury. As the Supreme Court has said, "Judicial scrutiny of counsel's performance must be highly deferential." Deferential, that is, to the lawyer's decision to do less than might be done or than the client would wish.

"Judicial scrutiny" will also be problematic. If the appointed lawyer who served at trial is also appointed on appeal, as is the norm, she is unlikely to argue that her own performance was deficient. Once the appeals are over, if the defendant figures out while sitting in jail that he did not receive counsel's effective assistance, he has no constitutional right at that point to a lawyer who will help him gather the facts and make those arguments. Once the direct appeals are over, the Supreme Court has held, the constitutional right to counsel evaporates.[38]

In *Gideon v. Wainwright*,[39] decided in 1962, the Supreme Court promised that all persons accused of a crime would have counsel. *Gideon*'s promise is largely unredeemed. However, there are thousands of courageous and diligent lawyers out there who are working long hours for their clients. There are law school clinical programs that provide trial, appellate, and post-conviction representation. You can see some of their work in highly publicized exonerations and acquittals. The dark side of that good news is that these successes uncover only a fraction of the systemic wrongs in the system that calls itself Justice.

PLEA BARGAINS: THE MYTHOLOGY OF CONSENT

More than 90 percent of those charged with crime make a bargain with the state to plead guilty to some charge or charges and conclude their case. Thus 90 percent or so of those in prison are there because, according to "the law," they agreed to be sent there.

This brings us to the contract that is related to that between the appointed lawyer and the client: the plea bargain.

A defendant is charged. The appointed lawyer points out that he could remain in jail and wait for trial, probably be convicted, and then spend significant jail time. On the other hand, a guilty plea will probably result in a lesser sentence, and even release for "time already served." Appointed counsel has a heavy case load and is likely to be drastically underfunded. Thus the "advice" about pleading guilty will too often be given without a thorough investigation of potential evidence, without demands that the state produce exculpatory evidence, and without systematic evaluation of factual and legal defenses that might be available.

The "contract" between the accused and the state follows a ritual form. The accused is asked if he understands the charges. At the lawyer's prodding, he says yes. The judge asks the accused if he wishes to waive a trial, and all the rights to summon and cross-examine witnesses that would be involved in a trial. The accused, often sensing that he has no realistic choice, says yes. The judge then seals the bargain and imposes sentence.

What's wrong with this picture? Two main things: the purported consent is unreal, and the accused is not truly informed of the rights he is forfeiting. First, the issue of *consent*: a free bargain requires freedom to choose, with knowledge of the rules at stake and the consequences. A prisoner being tortured may agree to make a statement, because he has no realistic choice. The worker may accept substandard working conditions because there is no other way to earn a wage. In the plea bargain setting, the lamentable quality of legal representation means that most indigent defendants cannot see any realistic way out of the plea bargain trap. To be sure, many defendants who plead guilty are in fact guilty and are saving the state the trouble of trying them. But every year a distressing number of cases come to light where defendants are railroaded into plea bargains. And even when a "guilty" defendant pleads, the lawyer's bad performance can result in a harsher sentence than would be received if the lawyer had aggressively and imaginatively presented evidence and argument in support of a lighter sentence. In some Western European countries, such as France, the system requires counsel to work hard on the issue of potential punishment, with a corresponding reduction in prison sentences and prison population.

Second, there is the issue of *informed* consent. The Supreme Court has held that the defendant entering a guilty plea need only be told of the *trial* rights that he is forfeiting, that is, of his right to summon witnesses and so on. In addition, he must be told of the maximum sentence. The Court has held that the defendant need not be told that he would have a right to challenge unlawful police activity, or other important procedural rights that supposedly restrain the state. Thus the defendant may never hear about how asserting those procedural rights could result in dismissal of the charges or a better bargain.

The newer wrinkle in all of this is the by-now-routine prosecution insistence that the defendant, as part of the bargain, affirmatively promises never to challenge the plea bargain as unfair. In ordinary commerce, this would be like buying a car after a strong sales pitch and, under pressure to purchase, being forced to agree that you could not bring the car back to the dealer even if it were lethally unsafe. Some appellate courts are questioning the validity of such agreements, but they are often, and perhaps mostly, upheld.[40] Professor Lon Fuller wrote in *The Morality of Law*: "It is vital that people understand the rules that are being applied to them." Did he ever spend a day in the criminal courts?

Supreme Court cases illustrate the mythology of free

bargain. In *Brady v. United States*,[41] the defendant pleaded guilty in 1959 to a federal kidnapping indictment and was sentenced to fifty years' imprisonment. Had he been found guilty by a jury, he might have received the death penalty, but the statute provided that the maximum punishment following a court trial or a guilty plea was life imprisonment. His plea colloquy included this exchange:

> **The Court:** You understand that . . . you are admitting and confessing the truth of the charge contained in the indictment and that you enter a plea of guilty voluntarily, without persuasion, coercion of any kind? Is that right?
>
> **Defendant Brady:** Yes, your Honor.

In 1967, while Brady was still in prison, the Supreme Court held in *United States v. Jackson* that the kidnapping statutory provision relating to the death penalty was unconstitutional. Brady sought to set aside his conviction. He argued that he made his plea bargain-to eliminate the unconstitutional risk of being executed.

The Supreme Court denied relief. Justice White, speaking for the Court, said, "The fact that the Federal Kidnapping Act tends to discourage defendants from insisting upon their innocence and demanding a trial by jury hardly implies that every defendant who enters a guilty plea to a charge under the Act does so involuntarily." Brady had admitted his factual guilt, and that was enough.

Justice White's analysis endorses a breathtaking theory of allegedly free bargain: a deal struck under an unconstitutionally generated fear of death passes the test of legitimacy. Equally significant, Justice White trashes the mythology of fair trial. Brady admitted he committed the alleged conduct;

no more questions need be asked. But wait a minute—the system of criminal law is hedged with constitutional provisions that protect against use of unlawfully obtained evidence, and provide for counsel, fair trial, and an impartial jury. The fundamental issue is not whether the accused "did the conduct," but whether the state can assemble lawful evidence that survives certain essential processes to exact punishment. Were it otherwise, we would brush aside all objections to punishing the defendant if only he or she would admit guilt.

Brady only wanted his alleged bargain declared void, so that he would not face further imprisonment unless the state proved him guilty. Or, once the bargaining started over on more equal terms, he could demand a lesser sentence than that imposed in the earlier proceeding.

Who is this being, who can divine that a criminal defendant threatened with the death penalty is really acting as a free agent? He is a Supreme Court Justice, who has never in his life faced such a decision, but will gladly imagine for us what it must be like.

Actually, I was on the same airplane flight as Justice White, many years ago. He was volubly distressed that the meal he had ordered had not made its way onto the airplane. If I had been quick-witted and brave, I could have explained to him: "Justice White, based on your own theory of contract, when you agreed with the airline to take this flight, you also agreed to endure all the unconcern, inefficiency and error that characterizes air travel. Anyhow, it is hardly a matter of life or death."

POINT: ORLANDO HALL, THE "OTHER," AND INEFFECTIVE COUNSEL

Orlando Hall, an African American, was convicted in 1995 of the drug-related kidnapping and murder of Lisa Rene. There is no doubt that he participated in the crime. The nature and degree of his participation is open to serious dispute. The principal evidence against him was provided by co-partici-pants acting under plea arrangements with the prosecutors, and by a jailhouse informant who claimed to have heard Mr. Hall make inculpatory statements. A federal jury sentenced Mr. Hall to death. He is on federal death row in Terre Haute, Indiana. As I write these words, his petition for review by the Inter-American Commission on Human Rights is pending.[42]

I learned about Mr. Hall's case when I became an expert witness for the defense, expressing the opinion that his appointed counsel had failed to fulfill their obligation. I testified to the Inter-American Commission that defense counsel's performance was so inadequate that Mr. Hall was denied fundamental rights under the American Convention on Human Rights. I see this case as another sorry chapter in this hemisphere's long history of subjugating and marginal-izing people of color.

The Supreme Court has held that no matter how horrific the crime, a defendant cannot be sentenced to death unless he or she has a meaningful opportunity to present mitigat-ing evidence. The sentencers must make a "reasoned moral response" to evidence about the offense and the offender.[43] In dozens of Supreme Court decisions, the Court's majority has held that imposition of the death penalty is constitutional because of all the Constitution-based "rights" of the accused in capital cases. Lawyers, scholars, and even some judges have seen past this mythology.[44]

The American Bar Association guidelines on capital rep-resentation tell counsel to do a prompt and thorough mitiga-tion investigation, going back at least three generations. The opportunity afforded by the law is illusory unless the lawyers investigate, find witnesses, and present evidence, and unless the trial judge admits that evidence and tells the jury to pay attention to it.

Mr. Hall's counsel did not begin their mitigation investigation until two and one-half weeks before trial. They were still doing that work during jury voir dire and opening statements, thus forfeiting the opportunity to make their questions to the prospective jurors and their initial discussion of the evidence pointedly relevant to Mr. Hall's circumstances.

The prosecutor in a capital case says to the jury, "Take this life. This person is the Other, unworthy of being in human society." A juror will not vote for that unless they truly believe that this is the "Other," unfit to live. When the defendant is already separated from the deciders—in this case an all-white jury—by the fact of his being African American, he is automatically at a disadvantage.

Mr. Hall's court-appointed lawyers came to the case as members of the dominant white culture. This separated them from their client, who grew up in a turbulent household, born into poverty in a racially striated community. His opportunities for self-transformation were constrained by a culture marked by generations of loss and hopelessness. Yet these lawyers did virtually nothing to overcome the barrier between themselves and him. They were going to present their arguments to this all-white jury, whose members were going to be as different from Mr. Hall as counsel themselves. After all, Mr. Hall's involvement in the events that led to the death here were not in dispute. He had surrendered and confessed without counsel. He had already begun to show remorse.

Defense counsel's tardy investigation was also cursory. They spent so little time visiting Mr. Hall's community, they could not possibly have gained the knowledge that they needed. This, even though the American Bar Association's guidelines tell us that there is this pivotal importance of using the investigation to develop the case. And they did nothing in the trial phase to lay out the basis for their later mitigation case.

These lawyers traduced their duty in at least four significant ways:

- First, the jury heard that Mr. Hall as a youngster was simply a witness to family violence. In fact, his father beat and raped his mother with the children waiting in the adjacent room to hear it. His father beat the children and told them that he'd brought them into the world and could take them out. The jury never heard this. A trauma specialist, Jill Miller showed that a full and proper investigation would have shown the jury that Mr. Hall was a victim of serious physical and mental abuse, yet trial counsel never saw the importance of getting an expert like Ms. Miller.

- Second, counsel ignored the indications that Mr. Hall had neuro-psychological deficits. They asked for appointment of an expert and then when the expert wasn't available they abandoned the plan.

- Third, counsel failed to investigate aspects of Mr. Hall's upbringing and culture. They had a preacher who knew him come to the trial, but they didn't even put him on the stand. This preacher would have discussed how an African American without economic opportunities could drift into the drug trade, how Mr. Hall perceived the need to support his siblings, and about Mr. Hall's remorse.

- Fourth, the lawyers failed to seek out potential evidence of Mr. Hall's good character, and of his good disciplinary record in prison. These may seem like minor issues, but in a federal death penalty case, the defendant's life is spared if just one juror finds a reason, any reason, to vote for life.

OBJECTIVELY INEFFECTIVE

When a defendant claims that his or her counsel was constitutionally "ineffective," the Supreme Court applies a test derived from *Strickland v. Washington*:

> A criminal defendant's Sixth Amendment right to counsel is violated if his trial attorney's performance falls below an objective standard of reasonableness and if there is a reasonable probability that the result of the trial would have been different absent the deficient act or omission.[45]

That word *objective* has been employed to deny relief to many defendants whose lawyers were shockingly inept and who made disastrous and often inexplicable choices. Reviewing courts have been ready to say that the lawyer was making "tactical" or "strategic" choices not to call available witnesses, to spend only limited time investigating the case, not probing prospective juror attitudes, and so on. The judges who excuse this lawyer behavior often have little trial experience or seem to believe that criminal defendants should receive legal services less adequate than corporate clients.

In 2000, a three-judge panel of the Fifth Circuit Court of Appeals ruled that Calvin Burdine's court-appointed counsel was not constitutionally ineffective. The lawyer, Joe Frank Cannon, frequently fell asleep during Burdine's capital trial. The court held that "it is impossible to determine—instead, only to speculate—that counsel's sleeping" harmed Burdine's case. The entire Fifth Circuit, fourteen judges, granted a rehearing and ruled 9 to 5 that "unconscious counsel equates to no counsel at all." Texas Attorney General John Cornyn asked the U.S. Supreme Court to reverse this holding and reinstate Burdine's death sentence. The Court declined review.[46]

While we may be heartened at the result, we must at the same time be concerned that agents of the state—elected prosecutors and appointed judges who dissented—could uphold the illusion of effective counsel in the face of the self-evident truth that a lawyer who is asleep will not be able to assert the defendant's rights.

What quality of representation could one expect in a system such as that in Texas, where lawyers who seek and obtain appointment in capital cases do not receive adequate compensation? As Judge Patrick Higginbotham said, ruling that a capital defendant's counsel was ineffective: "The state paid defense counsel $11.84 per hour. Unfortunately, the justice system got only what it paid for."[47] Later, Judge Higginbotham said he had changed his mind: the "justice system" did *not* get what it paid for.

Against this background, it was somewhat refreshing to read the Supreme Court's per curiam unanimous decision in *Hinton v. Alabama*.[48] Anthony Ray Hinton was charged with and convicted of murder and sentenced to death. The crucial evidence against him was a state crime laboratory ballistics test. That test concluded that a gun belonging to Mr. Hinton's mother—with whom he shared a home—had fired the bullets that killed the victims.

Defense counsel mistakenly believed that he could spend only $1,000 for an expert to rebut the state's conclusions. In fact, the statute on which he relied had been amended, and there was no cap on expenditures. Counsel, operating under this misimpression, could find only an expert who was not well-qualified and whose testimony counsel did not think was "effective." The Supreme Court held:

We do not today launch federal courts into examination of the relative qualifications of experts hired and experts that might have been hired. The only inadequate assistance of counsel here was the inexcusable mistake of law—the unreasonable failure to understand the resources that state law made available to him—that caused counsel to employ an expert that *he himself* deemed inadequate.

That is, the Court disavowed an intention that reviewing courts must parse expert testimony for its "quality." If counsel is free to choose an expert in a particular field and chooses a lousy one, the defendant may have no recourse.

Hinton identifies the key issue in ineffective assistance cases. One must get away from subjective analysis of counsel's decisions, for a reviewing court will be all too likely to indulge the myth that counsel's failure was the understandable result of deliberate choice. The challenge that faces the relevant constituencies is to articulate agreed standards of counsel conduct that can be held up as objective criteria. That work has begun and has gained the attention of courts.[49]

COUNTERPOINT: CLARENCE DARROW CONFRONTS RACIST MYTHOLOGY

I have been fascinated by the life and work of Clarence Darrow since I was a teenager. When I was eleven or twelve, my father gave me the Irving Stone biography, *Clarence Darrow for the Defense*. He told me that if I wanted to be a lawyer, I should be like Darrow—"He was for the people." I read Darrow's own memoir, other biographies of him, and collections of his jury speeches.[50] I wondered at how he wove together narratives about the social conditions of his time and the lives of defendants who were labor organizers, fighters for social change, and others targeted by the state and the wielders of economic power.

Darrow was lead trial counsel in the 1925–26 murder case brought against Dr. Ossian Sweet, an African-American physician in Detroit, and his family and friends.[51] Dr. Sweet bought a home for his family in an all-white Detroit neighborhood. A neighborhood association tried several stratagems to prevent the Sweets from moving in. Those failed, and the Sweet family took up residence. Fearing violence, the Sweets bought guns.

A white mob assembled at the Sweet home, throwing stones and chunks of coal at the house. Shots were fired from the Sweet home. One of the protesting mob, Leon Breiner, was hit and later died. Eleven people—members of the Sweet family and their friends—were charged with murder. The first trial, with all eleven defendants, ended with a hung jury and a mistrial. For the retrial, the prosecutors recognized that among the eleven defendants, there were at least some whose connection to the shots that killed Leon Breiner was at best tenuous. They decided to try Dr. Sweet alone. The jury acquitted him. The state did not retry the other defendants.

By 1925, Detroit's African-American population had dramatically increased. The Ku Klux Klan was active. There was a clear color line in housing, which the Klan and its allies worked to maintain.[52] Darrow took care to learn from and understand his clients and their community. He wrote in his memoir:

I had lived in America because I wanted to. Many others came here from choice to better their conditions. The ancestors of the negroes were captured in Africa and brought to America in slave ships, and had been obliged to toil for three hundred years without reward. When they were finally freed, from slavery they were lynched in court and out of court, burned at the stake, and driven into mean squalid outskirts and shanties.

In the first trial, Darrow made the defense opening statement to the jury after the prosecution had rested its case. In the second trial, he opened just after the prosecutor's opening statement. I believe that, on reflection, he concluded that the defense had to present its theory, and discuss defense evidence, as early as possible. Darrow could by this means advance alternatives to the prosecution's mythology-driven theory of the case. Darrow used the opening statement to set a scene—a white mob attacking a family exercising their right to live peaceably in their home.

Darrow confronted every prosecution witness with his or her sense of white privilege and power. His questions required the witnesses to admit that they opposed racial integration in housing, had no real contact with or knowledge about African Americans, and went along with what the "community" was doing. He had witnesses admit to being coached to deny that there had been a violent and angry mob in front of the Sweets' house. He showed that the police detachment that was supposed to protect the Sweets and their home did little to fulfill that duty. The defense team was ready to do this cross-examination because it had from first coming into the case done the hard work of fact investigation.

Darrow's decision to confront racist mythology with almost every witness was a necessary prelude to his closing argument. You cannot sum up a case you have not tried. The intellectual journey called "summation" amounts to revisiting the journey of the trial itself, organizing trial events, testimony, and exhibits into a coherent and persuasive pattern.

The basic theme of defense cross-examination, and the defense case, was founded on the idea of defending one's own home from attack and invasion. This too is a powerful mythology. Darrow had to build the factual case that would support its application to the Sweet family. Only then would he be able to argue that denying the benefit of this mythology to the Sweets could be based only on racial bias and prejudgment. Darrow began:

> Now, gentlemen, I say you are prejudiced. I fancy every one of you are, otherwise you would have some companions amongst these colored people. You will overcome it, I believe, in the trial of this case. But they tell me there is no race prejudice, and it is plain nonsense, and nothing else. Who are we, anyway? A child is born into this world without any knowledge of any sort. He has a brain which is a piece of putty; he inherits nothing in the way of knowledge or of ideas. If he is white, he knows nothing about color. He has no antipathy to the black.
>
> The black and the white both will live together and play together, but as soon as the baby is born we begin giving him ideas. We begin planting seeds in his mind. We begin telling him he must do this and he must not do that. We tell him about race and social equality and the thousands of things that men talk about until he grows up. It has been trained into us, and you, gentlemen, bring that feeling into this jury box, and that feeling which is a part of your lifelong training.
>
> You need not tell me you are not prejudiced. I know better. We are not very much but a bundle of

prejudices anyhow. We are prejudiced against other people's color. Prejudiced against other men's religion; prejudiced against other people's politics. Prejudiced against people's looks. Prejudiced about the way they dress. We are full of prejudices. You can teach a man anything beginning with the child; you can make anything out of him, and we are not responsible for it. Here and there some of us haven't any prejudices on some questions, but if you look deep enough you will find them; and we all know it.

All I hope for, gentlemen of the jury, is this: That you are strong enough, and honest enough, and decent enough to lay it aside in this case and decide it as you ought to. And I say, there is no man in Detroit that doesn't know that these defendants, every one of them, did right. There isn't a man in Detroit who doesn't know that the defendant did his duty, and that this case is an attempt to send him and his companions to prison because they defended their constitutional rights. It is a wicked attempt, and you are asked to be a party to it. You know it. I don't need to talk to this jury about the facts in this case.

There is no man who can read or can understand that does not know the facts. Is there prejudice in it? Now, let's see. I don't want to lean very much on your intelligence. I don't need much. I just need a little. Would this case be in this court if these defendants were not black? Would we be standing in front of you if these defendants were not black? Would anybody be asking you to send a boy to prison for life for defending his brother's home and protecting his own life, if his face wasn't black? What were the people in the neighborhood of Charlevoix and Garland

Streets doing on that fatal night? There isn't a child that doesn't know. Have you any doubt as to why they were there?

In the second trial, the prosecutors thought to make their strongest case by trying Dr. Sweet alone. But the lead prosecutor, Mr. Moll, could not resist claiming that Dr. Sweet and his family and friends were "all in it together," thus compounding the mythology of racism with that of conspiracy, the feeling of collective culpability that overrides any consideration of individual guilt.[53] Darrow took on both mythologies:

Was Mr. Moll right when he said that color has nothing to do with the case? There is nothing else in this case but the feeling of prejudice which has been carefully nourished by the white man until he doesn't know that he has it himself. While I admire and like my friend Moll very much, I can't help criticizing his argument. I suppose I may say what old men are apt to say, in a sort of patronizing way, that his zeal is due to youth and inexperience. That is about all we have to brag about as we get older, so we ought to be permitted to do that. Let us look at this case.

Mr. Moll took particular pains to say to you, gentlemen, that these eleven people here are guilty of murder; he calls this a cold-blooded, deliberate and premeditated murder; that is, they were there to kill. That was their purpose. Eleven, he said. I am not going to discuss the case of all of them just now, but I am starting where he started. He doesn't want any misunderstanding.

Amongst that eleven is Mrs. Sweet. The wife of Dr. Sweet, she is a murderer, gentlemen? The State's Attorney said so, and the Assistant State's Attorney said so. The State's Attorney would have to endorse it because he, himself, stands by what his assistant says. Pray, tell me what has Mrs. Sweet done to make her a murderer? She is the wife of Dr. Sweet. She is the mother of his little baby. She left the child at her mother's home while she moved into this highly cultured community near Goethe Street. Anyhow, the baby was to be safe; but she took her own chance, and she didn't have a gun; none was provided for her. Brother Toms drew from the witnesses that there were ten guns, and ten men. He didn't leave any for her. Maybe she had a pen knife, but there is no evidence on that question. What did she do, gentlemen? . . . She wasn't even upstairs. She didn't even look out of a window. She was down in the back kitchen cooking a ham to feed her family and friends, and a white mob came to drive them out of their home before the ham was served for dinner.

Darrow concluded: "Now, that is this case, gentlemen, and that is all there is to this case. Take the hatred away, and you have nothing left."

Of course, anyone who has kept up with events in Detroit knows that the Ossian Sweet trial victory did not obliterate racism in Detroit. I say again: We lawyers provide outcomes, not solutions. However, the outcome showed that white power could be resisted. And the organization around the trial, by the NAACP and others, helped foster the growth and development of a powerful movement.

ALBERT CAMUS'S *THE STRANGER*: MYTHOLOGIES OF TRIAL AND COLONIAL MENTALITY

In Albert Camus's 1942 novel *L'Étranger*, Meursault, a Frenchman, kills an Arab, is tried for murder, and is sentenced to death. The tribunal condemns him, or so it seems, because, as the prosecutor argues, he is not remorseful or compassionate, and is perhaps incapable of showing remorse. The United Kingdom editions of the novel in translation are titled *The Outsider*, which better evokes the book's theme. Meursault, particularly at his trial, is "outside" socially determined conventions. He is a defendant the state wishes to paint as "the Other," so that he may be condemned to death. In this view, Meursault evokes Roland Barthes's image of the state lending the accused a "spare brain," in order to condemn him "without remorse."

In 2015, the Algerian writer Kamel Daoud published a brilliant novel, *The Meursault Investigation*, in French, *Meursault, Contre-Enquête*. Daoud attacks the racism that he finds in Meursault's first-person account, and in the structure of Camus's novel.

So, we have before us two mythologies: One, from Camus's novel, is about the criminal law's indifference to the real events, motives, and emotions of those facing punishment. The other mythology, which Daoud exposes, is that of the colonial mentality, which sees the colonized as anonymous members of a subject people. On this view, Meursault's seeming lack of conscious concern for his Arab victim is not so much a personal failing as it is an inevitable part of the colonizers' mindset.

The Stranger begins: "*Aujourd'hui, maman est morte.*" Today, my mom is dead, or today my mom died. Meursault goes to the old-age home where his mother had been living and where she died. He declines to see her corpse and does not cry at her funeral.

The opening line is sometimes translated, "Mother died today." That translation, as some have noted, is wrong. "*Maman*" does not mean "mother." It is closer to "Mom" or even "Mommy." It does not mean just anyone's mother; it means the speaker's mother. It is a word that evokes a tender feeling. And the sentence should also be seen with the words in the proper order. Thus, "Today, my Mom died." To me, as to others, that opening sentence does bespeak the sense of loss that one has toward a parent one has loved. Meursault's lawyers could and should have begun with this bit of evidence and constructed a case in mitigation. Their failure was ineffective assistance of counsel, whether judged by contemporary U.S. standards or the rich tradition of French *avocats* and their *plaidoiries*.

Camus was asked what lesson one ought to draw from his book. He replied:

> "*Dans notre société*, tout homme qui ne pleure pas à l'enterrement de sa mère risque d'être condamné à mort." [In our society, any man who does not cry at his mother's funeral risks being condemned to death.] Years later, he explained: "*Je voulais dire seulement que le héros du livre est condamné parce qu'il ne joue pas le jeu.*" [I wanted to say only that the book's hero is condemned because he was not playing the game.]

Meursault's counsel did not play the trial game. Meursault was judged based on his and his advocate's unwillingness or inability to make the external expression of an internal feeling correspond to the dominant norm.

In the defense of capital cases, the lawyer's job is to change the focus of juror attention, to invite jurors to move beyond vengeance, to find a place from which to view the defendant and his actions.

In the Oklahoma City bombing case, Terry Nichols faced a possible jury verdict of death. Relatives and friends of victims testified at the penalty phase of his trial—angrily, tearfully, vengefully—all supporting the imposition of a death sentence. I spoke to the jurors:

> I feel now when I think about that evidence as though I'm standing before you and trying to sweep back a tide of anger and grief and vengeance. And I'm given pause by the fact that I feel that way, and I wonder if sometimes you might feel that way. But when I think that, then I think also of the instructions that the Judge is going to give you, because those instructions, as we contemplate this tide of anger and grief and vengeance, can get us all to higher ground, because the instructions will tell you that neither anger nor grief nor vengeance can ever be a part of a decision reached in a case of this kind.
>
> I am, when I say this, not attacking these victims. We know their sacrifice. But we know that with the centuries of our civilization piled so high that we have come a very long way from justice based on vengeance and blood feuds. This trial was moved from Oklahoma City because, I submit to you, it was thought that even the neighbors of those who lost so much would not do to sit in judgment. And to them, therefore, we can only say when we hear their grief and their anger and their desire for vengeance, "Bless those in need of healing." . . . I want to share with you some thoughts about a concept of justice, to share

with you some thoughts that suggest that if you come to this point you would turn your face toward the future and not toward the past.

In that trial, as in Meursault's trial, the state invited the deciders to accept a mythology about just deserts and punishment. The use of such mythologies is always an invitation, sometimes a demand, that people see events in a certain way, and conclude that this is the way the world ought to be. Busting the mythologies imposed by wielders of public and private power involves redirecting people's consciousness in at least two ways. First, we present evidence that undermines a mythology's perceived legitimacy and application. Second, we may present an alternative way of organizing consciousness. In order to ask the jurors to direct their attention in a certain way, we must give them something concrete, some evidence, at which to look.

We deal with the world based on our conscious perception of what is going on. That perception is, in turn, influenced by how we direct our attention, or have it directed for us by someone else. This is the process that Jean-Paul Sartre wrote of in *Being and Nothingness*:

But if we wish to decide with assurance, we have only to consider an example of a negative judgment and to ask ourselves whether it causes non-being to appear at the heart of the being, or merely limits itself to some earlier discovery. I have an appointment with Pierre at four o'clock. I arrive at the café a quarter of an hour late; Pierre is always punctual; will he have waited for me? I look at the room, the patrons, and I say, "He is not here." Is there an intuition of Pierre's absence, or rather does the negation enter in only with judgment?

At first sight, it seems absurd to speak here of intuition because, to be precise, there could not be an intuition of nothing and because the absence of Pierre is this nothing. Popular consciousness, however, bears witness to this intuition. Do we not say, for example, "I immediately saw that he was not there." Is this simply a matter of misplacing the negation? Let us look a little closer.

It is certain that the café by itself, with its patrons, its tables, its booths, its mirrors, its light, its smoky atmosphere, and the noise of voices, rattling saucers, and footsteps that fill it—the café is a fullness of being. And all the intuitions of detail that I might have are filled by these odors, these sounds, these colors, all phenomena that have a transphenomenal being. Similarly, Pierre's actual presence in a place that I do not know is a plenitude of being. We seem to have found fullness everywhere. But one must observe that in perception there is always the construction of a figure on a ground. No one object, no group of objects is especially designed to be organized as specifically either ground or figure; *all depends on the direction of my attention*. When I enter this café to look for Pierre, there is formed a synthetic organization of all the objects in the café, on the ground of which Pierre is given as about to appear.

Camus invites us to see Meursault as an alienated individual who kills someone and who might have escaped a death sentence if he and his lawyers had been willing to use the tools of evidence and persuasion that the trial process made available to them. This would have been "playing the game."

Because Camus's novel is written in the first person, we

are invited to see Algeria as Meursault sees it. Meursault's attention is directed by his creator. Camus was born in 1913, in the French colony of Algeria. The official French designation was that Algeria was an "overseas department" (*département d'outre-mer*) of France, a form of words designed to defy the reality of colonial rule.[54]

In *The Stranger,* none of the Arab characters, including Meursault's victim, has a name. Daoud's novel is narrated by Harun, an Algerian man, who tells us that Meursault killed his brother Musa, and reproaches Meursault for dehumanizing the colonized Algerians. Portrayed by Daoud, Meursault is not a lonely alienated individual who stumbles into a criminal act, and who perhaps lacks the usual capacity for remorse and compassion. No, we must see Meursault as emblematic of the colonial French. He may indeed have had sadness at his mother's death, but he regards the life—better, perhaps, the human existence—of a young Arab man as not worth caring about. We are reminded of Black youths cut down by police gunfire.

Daoud is a myth-buster. He shows us that Camus's focus on an individual crime in a French colony, in a story where none of the Arabs have names, masks the reality of colonial life. Meursault's trial was, therefore, a "game" in two senses. First, Meursault and his lawyers did not use the law's tools to paint a picture of Meursault as having human qualities. Second, Daoud reminds us, the crime and its treatment by the forces of order was wrongly portrayed as a rather banal homicide.

Camus, the Nobel laureate, is generally despised in Algeria, and not as a matter of literary taste. He argued that Algeria should "remain part of France," thus embracing the mythology of "*département d'outre-mer.*" This was a lacuna in his vision, for he surely understood and despised the racist savagery of the Nazis. He wrote to a German friend just after the Second World War:

> Qu'est-ce sauver l'homme? Mais je vous le crie de tout moi-même, c'est de ne pas le mutiler et c'est donner ses chances à la justice, qu'il est le seul à concevoir.[55]

> [What is it that will save man? I cry out with all my being, it is that he is not mutilated, and that he is given his chance for justice, which he is the sole being to have conceived.]

BATTLING FOR DEFENDANT RIGHTS

We are shoveling people into the prisons at an enormous rate. We could call this process "overcriminalization," but that name seems to mask rather than illuminate the root causes. What means are there to expose the systematic injustices? How can we expose the phony bargains between lawyer and client and between client and the state? What moves the system in this direction? And is effective counsel simply a dream?

The system moves in this way because it is designed to serve the interests of the dominant class. The essays in the next three chapters underscore this point.

Lawyers, to a distressing extent, are not moved to lead the resistance. Lawyers neither own the means of production nor labor in ways that supply them with class consciousness. People of color are underrepresented in the ranks of lawyers, and only in the past twenty years has any significant number of Hispanic lawyers entered the profession. Once in the legal profession, people of color tend to be relegated to its lowest rungs and face race-based obstacles to advancement.

One ticket to advancement is to abandon the cause of racial justice. Law school programs designed to redress historic inequality are increasingly under attack.

Lawyers consume surplus value, and those with surplus value to distribute are mainly on the side of this repressive system. Labor organizations also hire lawyers, but the valiant work of these lawyers deals mostly with workers' rights and not criminal justice.

As in times past, however, lawyers overcome their class-based bias and obliquity. They enter the struggle for change. In *Law and the Rise of Capitalism*, I discussed the role and importance of such lawyers. They do not stand at the center of events, but they assist those who are at the center or who are brought into conflict with the state. Lawyers help to turn claims for justice into coherent demands and principles. They may show the open spaces within an old system, where change can be successful. When the open spaces close, they can help define the conditions on which a new order will be created.

Some question my picture of lawyers' potential role. Yet, in struggle after struggle, fighters for justice have drawn on legal ideology. Nelson Mandela and Oliver Tambo were lawyers, and their continued calls for justice were phrased in terms of the legal ideology that would emerge in a transformed South Africa. Honorable public defenders and appointed counsel, of whom there are many, fight the system one battle at a time. We salute them, while remembering Yevtushenko's words:

> *How sharply our children will be ashamed*
> *Taking at last their vengeance for these horrors*
> *That in so strange a time*
> *Common integrity could look like courage*

In some law schools, such as Washington College of Law at American University, where I teach, clinical legal education helps to prepare lawyers to meet the challenges that this system poses. Nationally, only about 3 percent of law graduates go into public interest law, compared with some 15 percent twenty-five years ago. At WCL, we manage to place about three times the national average in such jobs. Restrictions on funding for defender services, state and federal, have eroded the job opportunities in that sector. Meanwhile, the law graduate who goes into public interest work will earn less than 20 percent of what a graduate who enters private practice can expect. Twenty-five years ago, the disparity was much less—about half. Concerned law students should join with such progressive organizations as the National Lawyers Guild.

Human rights organizations have creatively attacked the system's unfairness by class action lawsuits that further the demands of many defendants and target entire jail or prosecutorial systems. For example, the Southern Center for Human Rights under the leadership of Stephen Bright has effectively litigated for better medical care, and better access to counsel to make bail motions. Similar lawsuits have been brought by the Prisoners' Rights Project and the Center for Constitutional Rights.

The scandalous lack of adequate counsel can never be solved by piecemeal litigation of individual clients' claims of ineffective assistance. Rather, all the constituencies must look to the direct action and litigation strategies of the civil rights movement. Litigation strategy will include class action lawsuits. The basic point must be that chronically underfunded efforts are per se unacceptable, as they provide an inherent disincentive to good lawyering. One way to force reform of our system of locking up so many people is to make the instruments of state power appreciate and pay the constitutionally mandated costs of such a decision. That is, the Constitution is mocked by the state spending millions for prisons and providing derisory sums to defend those the state wants to put behind bars.

The large-scale class action is significant for the same reason that civil rights litigation of the 1940s, 1950s, and 1960s played such a constructive role. Given the real world of conservative judges, this kind of litigation faces significant obstacles to courtroom success. Like much class suit litigation, however, the lawsuit can serve as a means to focus public attention on issues. It can and should be part of a broader organizing effort. In this arena as in others, the community's demands and needs, and not the lawyer's view of the world, should have pride of place.

Forms of resistance that focus on courtrooms may be useful, but ultimately they lead to palliative solutions. "From such resistance may come consciousness of a need for fundamental social change." Ralph Waldo Emerson asked Henry David Thoreau, "What branches of learning did you find at Harvard?" Thoreau replied, "All of the branches and none of the roots." We can work on the branches, but we need to get to the roots.

— 3 —

Mythologies of Free Expression

THE MARKETPLACE OF IDEAS

I WENT DOWN TO THE MARKETPLACE of ideas the other day, but they didn't have anything I was interested in. Used to be they had some specialty stores with really neat ideas that you could pick up and actually use to make stuff—like social change. That was before they moved the marketplace out of downtown and into a mall dominated by big-box stores.

When I got to the marketplace, there were bunches of people who had set up stands in the parking lot and were offering really interesting, challenging ideas. But the cops were running them off. I hear that there are still some small stores with good ideas, so I will be going back this week to check that out.

The mythology of free speech sustains the mythology of democratic government. A free people live under laws made by a process in which they make free choices based on the free flow of information that is discussed and weighed in an open public forum.

Today's mythology of free speech begins with John Milton's *Areopagitica*, an address delivered in 1644, attacking official and ecclesiastical censorship. Milton argued the value of the free flow of ideas and information:

I cannot praise a fugitive and cloistered virtue, un-exercised and unbreathed, that never sallies out and sees her adversary but slinks out of the race, where that immortal garland is to be run for, not without dust and heat. Assuredly we bring not innocence into the world, we bring impurity much rather; that which purifies us is trial, and trial is by what is contrary. . . .

. . . And though all the winds of doctrine were let loose to play upon the earth, so Truth be in the field, we do injuriously, by licensing and prohibiting, to misdoubt her strength. Let her and Falsehood grapple; who ever knew Truth put to the worse, in a free and open encounter?

This idea of a "free and open encounter" lies behind the First Amendment to the United States Constitution:

Congress shall make no law respecting an estab-lishment of religion, or prohibiting the free exercise thereof; or abridging the freedom of speech, or of the press; or the right of the people peaceably to assem-ble, and to petition the Government for a redress of grievances.

James Madison wrote:
Knowledge will forever govern ignorance. And a peo-ple who mean to be their own governor must arm themselves with the power that knowledge gives. A popular government without popular information or the means for acquiring it is but a prologue to a farce or tragedy or perhaps both.

John Adams wrote:

> And liberty can not be preserved without a general
> knowledge. But besides this they have a right, an un-
> disputable, unalienable, indefeasible divine right to
> the most dreaded and most envied kind of knowledge,
> I mean of the characters and conduct of their rulers.

The mythology of the marketplace of ideas—free expression and its role in self-government and in people's right to
make intelligent choices—has been undermined in four significant ways: state repression, concentrated control of the
technological means of communication, invocation of the
private property norm, and the wholesale characterization
of information as a form of property. The state's overt role
in repressing speech operates visibly. The ways in which
monopolization and the enforcement of the private property
norm operate to curtail the marketplace of ideas may be less
obvious to us.

STATE REPRESSION

In the early twentieth century, the rise of socialist, labor, and
antiwar movements provoked prosecutions for criminal syndicalism and sedition. Justice Oliver Wendell Holmes Jr. dissented in one such case, speaking of the "free trade in ideas"
in "the competition of the market," hitching a mythology of
free speech to the mythology of capitalist social relations.
Dissenting in a criminal syndicalism case in 1927, Justice
Louis Brandeis argued that the remedy for speech that is
troubling is "more speech, not enforced silence." In a 1953
case, Justice William O. Douglas spoke of "bidding for the
minds of men in the marketplace of ideas."

Despite these bold references, the state prosecuted people for speech that was said to threaten the established order,

and by this means removed some purveyors from the marketplace and discouraged others from entering it. Legislative committees pilloried dissidents, seeking to delegitimize some market participants and their ideas. Militant labor unions were marginalized. Dissenters were hounded from public and private employment.

Underlying the repression was an orchestrated fear of the social change that free speech might engender. Often, the fear was stoked by the state's claims that the dangerous speech was being dictated by foreign ideologies. During the 1930s, in California, farm labor organizers were prosecuted for criminal syndicalism. The Hearst newspapers supplied local district attorneys with an "expert" witness who would testify that the defendants' doctrine was based on Soviet-style Communism. Lincoln Steffens's son Pete, who attended some of the trials, recalls the cross-examination of one such witness:

> **Q:** You are familiar with the teachings of Karl Marx?
> **A:** Yes
> **Q:** Can you define "dialectical materialism"?
> **A:** Well (pausing), you have to take it one word at a time. "Dialect"—that's the way that foreigners talk. And "materialism," that means going after money. So "dialectical materialism" is a bunch of foreigners who are trying to take our money.

Civil liberties litigation in the 1960s and onward went some way toward restoring free expression to the marketplace, following the chilling effect of McCarthyism.

WHO OWNS THE STREETS?

In towns across the country, local cops arrested labor organizers and itinerant preachers. In the 1930s and 1940s, the United States Supreme Court decided a few cases that honored the idea of a marketplace where information and ideas might be exchanged.

In *Hague v. CIO*,[56] the Supreme Court invalidated a city ordinance that gave the chief of police unregulated discretion to deny permits to hold gatherings in the streets and parks. The petitioners were seeking to inform workers about the National Labor Relations Act. Hague was "Boss" Frank Hague, mayor of Jersey City from 1917 to 1947. During the 1930s, Hague used the police force to roust, arrest, kidnap, and attack CIO organizers and their allies. Justices Roberts and Black said this about the state's claim that the streets and parks were its property:

> Wherever the title of streets and parks may rest, they have immemorially been held in trust for the use of the public and, time out of mind, have been used for purposes of assembly, communicating thoughts between citizens, and discussing public questions. Such use of the streets and public places has, from ancient times, been a part of the privileges, immunities, rights, and liberties of citizens. The privilege of a citizen of the United States to use the streets and parks for communication of views on national questions may be regulated in the interest of all; it is not absolute, but relative, and must be exercised in subordination to the

general comfort and convenience, and in consonance with peace and good order; but it must not, in the guise of regulation, be abridged or denied.

The Court confronted the property norm again in a 1946 case, *Marsh v. Alabama*.[57] Chickasaw, Alabama., a suburb of Mobile, was a company town owned by Gulf Shipbuilding. It had houses, stores, a post office, and all the other characteristics of a town, but all of this sat on land owned by Gulf Shipbuilding. Grace Marsh was a Jehovah's Witness. She stood on the sidewalk near the Chickasaw post office

> and undertook to distribute religious literature. In the stores the corporation had posted a notice which read as follows: "This Is Private Property, and Without Written Permission, No Street, or House Vendor, Agent or Solicitation of Any Kind Will Be Permitted." [Ms. Marsh] was warned that she could not distribute the literature without a permit and told that no permit would be issued to her.

Ms. Marsh was charged with trespass. The Alabama courts upheld the conviction. The Supreme Court reversed. Justice Black, for the five-justice Supreme Court majority, wrote:

> We do not agree that the corporation's property interests settle the question. The State urges in effect that the corporation's right to control the inhabitants of Chickasaw is coextensive with the right of a homeowner to regulate the conduct of his guests. We can not accept that contention. Ownership does not always mean absolute dominion. The more an owner,

for his advantage, opens up his property for use by the
public in general, the more do his rights become cir-
cumscribed by the statutory and constitutional rights
of those who use it.

It might have seemed, reading such cases as *Marsh* and
Hague, that the mythology of the marketplace could in some
measure come true. The Court's decision in *Marsh* embraced
the idea of functional reality. Gulf Shipbuilding had made
Chickasaw look like a town, with streets and shops and places where people would congregate. Therefore, it should serve
the social function of a town.

Ms. Marsh preached religious doctrine. The organizers
in *Hague* urged workers to unite. Other speakers in these
marketplaces of ideas advanced political ideas about social
change. The value of their speech depended on being able to
reach an audience.

Out in California, after the Second World War, the population expansion led to the creation of vast suburbs and, to
serve these populations, shopping malls. A mall sits in the
middle of a vast space. It is surrounded with parking lots.
Inside the mall are large and small retail stores. In the mall
are workers who sell the goods in the stores, cook the food
sold in the food court, clean the restrooms, and do the other
jobs that keep the enterprise functioning. These workers are
among the lowest-paid members of the labor force.

Population density in suburbia is much less than in the
central city. And many suburbs are destinations for white
flight. These shopping malls are among the few places where
people congregate in suburbia.

In suburban Los Angeles, a shopping mall arose in
the early 1960s. In the mall was a bakery where wages
and working conditions were substandard. The Bakery &

Confectionery Workers Union began to hold informational picketing just outside the bakery, on sidewalks that were the property of the mall owner, Schwartz-Torrance Investment Company. The owner sued to enjoin the picketing. The California Supreme Court saw the case like this:

> Picketing by a labor union constitutes an integral component of the process of collective bargaining; as such, it involves the exercise of a right which is both statutorily and constitutionally sanctioned. On the other hand, the countervailing interest which plaintiff endeavors to vindicate emanates from the exclusive possession and enjoyment of private property. Because of the public character of the shopping center, however, the impairment of plaintiff's interest must be largely theoretical. Plaintiff has fully opened his property to the public. Approximately 10,000 people visit the premises weekly. The shopping center affords unrestricted access between its parking lot and the public streets. The center constitutes a conglomeration of business enterprises designed to provide essential services to all members of the local community; "Access by the public is the very reason for its existence." [58]

"Very reason" might summon up an image of the mall as simulacrum of the central city that the mall displaced, as a mythological image of people gathering to engage in aspects of social existence. This relatively indeterminate image of people exchanging ideas soon yielded to the determinate and fixed private property norm.

In 1968, the United States Supreme Court addressed the same issue. The Logan Valley Mall, near Altoona, Pennsylvania, had a Weis supermarket among its tenants. All the

Weis employees were non-union. As part of an organizing drive, the Amalgamated Food Employees Union held an informational picket on the sidewalk outside the Weis store, on property owned by the mall developer. Justice Marshall, writing for six justices, began by noting that picketing, like the handbilling in which Ms. Marsh had been engaged, is entitled to First Amendment protection. Adopting the rationale of *Marsh* and the California mall case, Justice Marshall held:

> Here the roadways provided for vehicular movement within the mall and the sidewalks leading from building to building are the functional equivalents of the streets and sidewalks of a normal municipal business district. The shopping center premises are open to the public to the same extent as the commercial center of a normal town. . . . The State may not delegate the power, through the use of its trespass laws, wholly to exclude those members of the public wishing to exercise their First Amendment rights on the premises in a manner and for a purpose generally consonant with the use to which the property is actually put.[59]

Justice Black, who had written one of the lead opinions in *Marsh*, was among the dissenters. He declined to accept what he viewed as an extension of the *Marsh* principle. Private property, which includes the owner's right to exclude people from entering, is also a Constitution-based value. He then wrote:

> Of course there was an implicit invitation for customers of the adjacent stores to come and use the marked-off places for cars. But the whole public was no more

wanted there than they would be invited to park free at a pay parking lot. Is a store owner or are several owners together less entitled to have a parking lot set aside for customers than other property owners? To hold that store owners are compelled by law to supply picketing areas for pickets to drive store customers away is to create a court-made law wholly disregarding the constitutional basis on which private ownership of property rests in this country.

This statement, by a justice celebrated for upholding the First Amendment rights of speech, press, and association, should give us pause. On the one hand, Justice Black elevates property ownership to a constitutional status that it has never been held to possess. The mall developer suffered all manner of limits on what it could do with its property, including zoning, parking limitations, extent of impervious cover, access for emergency vehicles, and so on. On the other hand, Justice Black equates his hitherto precious First Amendment to the right to park one's car. The First Amendment may now be likened to man's eternal search for a parking meter with time left on it.

By 1972, the Court's membership had changed. In *Lloyd Corporation v. Tanner*,[60] the mall owner won. An antiwar group wanted to distribute handbills inside a cavernous mall in Portland, Oregon.

Lloyd Corp., Ltd., owns a large, modern retail shopping center in Portland, Oregon. Lloyd Center embraces altogether about 50 acres, including some 20 acres of open and covered parking facilities which accommodate more than 1,000 automobiles. It has a perimeter of almost one and one-half miles, bounded by four public streets. It is crossed in varying degrees by several other public streets, all of which have adjacent public sidewalks. Lloyd owns all land and buildings within the Center, except these public streets and sidewalks. There are some 60 commercial tenants, including small shops and several major department stores.

The decision was 5–4. For the majority, Justice Powell wrote:

The handbilling by respondents in the malls of Lloyd Center had no relation to any purpose for which the center was built and being used. It is nevertheless argued by respondents that, since the Center is open to the public, the private owner can not enforce a restriction against handbilling on the premises. The thrust of this argument is considerably broader than the rationale of *Logan Valley*. It requires no relationship, direct or indirect, between the purpose of the expressive activity and the business of the shopping center. The message sought to be conveyed by respondents was directed to all members of the public, not solely to patrons of Lloyd Center or of any of its operations. Respondents could have distributed these handbills on any public street, on any public sidewalk, in any public park, or in any public building in the city of Portland.

Respondents' argument, even if otherwise meritorious, misapprehends the scope of the invitation extended to the public. The invitation is to come to the Center to do business with the tenants. It is true that facilities at the Center are used for certain meetings and for various promotional activities. The obvious

purpose, recognized widely as legitimate and responsible business activity, is to bring potential shoppers
to the Center, to create a favorable impression, and
to generate goodwill. There is no open-ended invitation to the public to use the Center for any and all
purposes.

If you listen carefully, you can hear a requiem for *Logan
Valley*. If you thought you heard that, you would be right.
In 1976, *Hudgens v. National Relations Board*[61] came before
the Court. A labor union representing warehouse employees
was on strike against one of the mall tenants, and it set up
picket lines in the mall. The Court expressly overruled *Logan
Valley*, 6–2, Justice Stevens not sitting. The Court held: "The
Constitution by no means requires such an attenuated doctrine of dedication of private property to public use."

To drive home the point, the Court held: "The constitutional guarantee of free expression has no part to play in a
case such as this." That is, freedom of expression has nothing
to do with people who feel free to express themselves. If we
recur to the "balance" metaphor of *Marsh* and *Schwartz-Torrance*, the playground bully has pushed free expression off
the seesaw.

There was a small and grudging victory for the marketplace mythology in 1980.[62] The factual setting resembled that
of the earlier cases:

Appellant PruneYard is a privately owned shopping
center in the city of Campbell, Cal. It covers ap-
proximately 21 acres—5 devoted to parking and 16
occupied by walkways, plazas, sidewalks, and buildings that contain more than 65 specialty shops, 10
restaurants, and a movie theater. . . . It has a policy

> not to permit any visitor or tenant to engage in any
> publicly expressive activity, including the circulation
> of petitions, that is not directly related to its commer-
> cial purposes. . . . Appellees are high school students
> who sought to solicit support for their opposition to
> a United Nations resolution against "Zionism." On a
> Saturday afternoon they set up a card table in a cor-
> ner of PruneYard's central courtyard. They distribut-
> ed pamphlets and asked passersby to sign petitions,
> which were to be sent to the President and Members
> of Congress. Their activity was peaceful and orderly
> and so far as the record indicates was not objected to
> by PruneYard's patrons.

Mall security guards told the students to leave. They left, and filed suit. The California Supreme Court adhered to its holding in the *Schwartz-Torrance* case, but expressly rested its decision on the California state constitution's free speech guarantee. The United States Supreme Court has no power to tell a state how to interpret its own constitution, so the mall developer argued that permitting leafleting on its pri-vate property was a taking of private property and therefore a violation of the federal Constitution. No, said a unanimous Supreme Court in *PruneYard Shopping Center v. Robins*. All that language in prior opinions about property rights could not be taken to deprive states of the power to impose reason-able restrictions on the uses to which property might be put.

Other states have declined to go along with California's view of matters.[63] For example, the Minnesota Supreme Court held in 1999 that there is no constitutional right of free expres-sion in and around the Mall of America. The Mall of Amer-ica is 1.15 miles long, and has an amusement park, a theater, an aquarium, restaurants, a transit station, and many other attractions in addition to retail stores. It attracts 42 million annual visitors. But there is no marketplace of ideas there.

The marketplace of ideas had become the shopping mall of ideas. The selection of available ideas was limited at best. Justice Brandeis's view that the answer to disturbing speech is "more speech" was overrun by the right of property.

The judges, justices, and lawyers who viewed the right of property as a right to exclude were, whether consciously or not, expressing the basic principle of the bourgeois real property norm. This norm had begun to find expression in the sixteenth century and was by the nineteenth century observable in a fully developed form. Its mythology is rooted in the idea that a private person has no social obligation with respect to the goods he owns. The goods are impersonal, and all the property owner desires is the "same" right of exclusive dominion that "everybody" has.

But For Colporteurs, Maybe Anything Goes

By the mid-1500s, the number of people in Europe who could read had greatly increased. A century earlier, Johannes Gutenberg had introduced moveable type. These were ingredients from which a publishing industry might be fashioned. There was a great increase in the number of peddlers, carrying religious tracts for sale from place to place. The French designation for these peddlers, "colporteur," came into general usage.

In the United States, beginning in the 1800s, colporteurs went door-to-door selling or giving away not only religious literature but political tracts as well. The most famous publisher of inexpensive political books was the socialist activist Emanuel Haldeman-Julius. The "Little Blue Books" that his company published sold millions of copies in the early twentieth century. Haldeman-Julius reprinted an array of progressive literature, from Clarence Darrow's summations in labor rights cases, to works on economics, to the poetry of Walt Whitman.

Like the speakers in marketplaces, colporteurs needed access to an audience. Towns and cities began to restrict and regulate their activity. Advocates for secular as well as religious causes were held to have a First Amendment right to knock on doors and hand out literature. As the Supreme Court held in a 1939 case:

> Municipal authorities . . . have the duty to keep their communities' streets open and available for movement of people and property, the primary purpose to which the streets are dedicated. So long as legislation to this end does not abridge the constitutional liberty of one rightfully upon the street to impart information through speech or the distribution of literature, it may lawfully regulate the conduct of those using the streets. . . . Pamphlets have proved most effective instruments in the dissemination of opinion. And perhaps the most effective way of bringing them to the notice of individuals is their distribution at the homes of the people. On this method of communication the ordinance imposes censorship, abuse of which engendered the struggle in England which eventuated in the establishment of the doctrine of the freedom of the press embodied in our Constitution. To require a censorship through license which makes impossible the free and unhampered distribution of pamphlets strikes at the very heart of the constitutional guarantees.[64]

In recent years, the exercise of this freedom has been

chilled. A homeowner behind that door might be fearful—
and armed. Apartment buildings in "nice" neighborhoods
are sealed off by electronic front-door locks or guarded
by a doorman. Most significantly, those with means have
embraced the same property norm that guided the Supreme
Court's shopping mall decisions. They have moved behind
gates, fences, and walls. Professor Setha Low's compelling
book, *Behind the Gates: Life, Security, and the Pursuit of
Happiness in Fortress America*, tells stories of people moving
into these walled cities, where their fears of "the Other" are
calmed and they learn to live in isolation from the tumult of
the marketplace of ideas.

Sometimes buyers learn that their enclave has problems
of its own, often because the developer's sense of responsibility is also dictated by the desire to accumulate wealth. A
taxi was taking me to the airport, and we drove past a gated
community in the marshland of eastern North Carolina, far
from the problems of urban living. "See that," he said. "It's a
swamp. But if you put eighteen inches of dirt on it, you can
sell it to Yankees."

Abolishing "Feudalism": A Mythology of Freedom

The private property norm, wielded by judges on behalf of
owners, dissipates the mythology of "free government by free
men," animated by the free exchange of information and ideas.
The notion of "private" property traces deep historical roots.[65]

In the feudal period, use of land was regulated by the
relationship of a secular or ecclesiastical overlord or seigneur
and the vassals who pledged homage to him. In the part of
Europe once ruled from Rome, feudalism represented the
retreat into the manor and village of a ruling class deprived
of protection by a decayed and dying imperial government.

Elsewhere, it was a change from a pastoral, nomadic, and war-directed existence to a more stable agricultural life (although still warlike enough). The various measures of land are one witness to the principal economic concern of the manor, for the standard, whether the *mansio* of Gaul or the "hide" of England, was that which could support one family, and its size varied depending on the region and the fertility of the soil.

At the root of the feudal relation was the act of homage, supplemented from the time of Charlemagne in the ninth century by the oath of fealty. Two men, one stronger (the lord), the other weaker (the vassal), face each other. As the French historian Marc Bloch describes it, the latter puts his hands together and places them, thus joined, between the hands of the other man—a plain symbol of submission, the significance of which was sometimes further emphasized by a kneeling posture. At the same time, the person proffering his hands utters a few words—a very short declaration—by which he acknowledges himself to be the "man" of the person facing him. Then chief and subordinate kiss each other on the mouth, symbolizing accord and friendship. Such were the simple gestures, eminently fitted to make an impression on minds so sensitive to visible things, that served to cement one of the strongest social bonds known in the feudal era.

The essence of the feudal relation was this personal nexus, originally enduring only for the lifetime of the vassal, and later extended to the vassal's heirs in the male line. For the vassal held the land he tilled, and virtually all his movable possessions, "of" his lord. The oath-bound relation of dominance and subordination, from the tiller to his lord, and through the latter's pledge of homage to some more powerful seigneur, constituted a system often described by its ideologists in pyramidal, symmetrical terms.

Few lived outside the feudal system. The Church participated, as feudal lord. Local priests were attached to a village
or manor. Those who did not live in homage of mouth and
hands were few—pilgrims, wandering friars, itinerant merchants, troubadours, and other social outcasts.

The feudal notion of property regarded landholding as
carrying certain responsibilities. R. H. Tawney wrote, in *Religion and the Rise of Capitalism*:

> Property is not a mere aggregate of economic privi-
> leges, but a responsible office. Its raison d'être is not
> only income, but service. It is to secure its owner such
> means, and no more than such means, as may en-
> able him to perform those duties, whether labor on
> the land, or labor in government, which are involved
> in particular status which he holds in the system. He
> who seeks more robs his superiors, or his dependents,
> or both. He who exploits his property with a single
> eye to its economic possibilities at once perverts its
> very essence and destroys his own moral tide, for he
> has "every man's living and does no man's duty."[66]

With this notion went that of nonexclusivity—land might
be held in common, or a piece of land might be used at different seasons by different persons for the benefit of the community. Peasant subsistence was based on tillage of particular land, pasturage, and tillage of land regarded as common,
as were hunting and gathering in woods and forests.

Tawney's characterization of this system as having a
rough equity is in some measure right, but it also suggests
a romantic mythology of feudalism. The set of customary
rights and duties that characterized vassalage were, at best,
designed to promote the lord's profit and the peasant's mere

survival. The peasant's custom-based rights were often won and then defended with sanguinary social struggle.

The erosion and overthrow of feudal relationships, largely coeval with the consolidation of state power into nation-states, was accompanied by the introduction of the bourgeois property norm. As expressed by Karl Renner, in *The Institutions of Private Law and Their Social Functions*:

> The right of ownership, dominium, is a person's all-embracing legal power over a tangible object. As far as the object is concerned, ownership is a universal institution: all corporeal things, even land, can be objects of ownership if they are recognized as such by the law and are not by special provision put *extra commercium*. Ownership is equally universal with regard to the subject. Everybody has an equal capacity for ownership, and he may own property of every description. These are the norms which are characteristic of this institution.[67]

Thus the institution of property in the sense it came to have in bourgeois law posits a person (*persona*) and a thing (*res*), joined by the legal norm called property or ownership. Human society is dissolved into isolated individuals, and the world of goods split up into discrete items. One can no longer speak of a duty to use property or behave toward others in a certain way: all such duties as may be imposed by law are prima facie derogations from the fundamental "right of property."

In this description of the bourgeois property norm lies the mythology I have been discussing: the right of property does not involve any domination of a person by another person. It is simply a relation between a person and a thing.

And if the "thing" is a shopping center where you want to hand out leaflets as you would do in a downtown shopping area with discrete shops, the real-world suppression of your freedom of expression is masked by invocation of the mythological person-thing relationship. The formulation of the property norm as "person" and "thing" was proclaimed by seventeenth- and eighteenth-century philosophers as a natural right.

The property norm did not arise by itself and take its place in the pantheon of legal ideology. Its legal form was enacted, wielded, and enforced to foster a system of social relations whose control over the means of production and exchange was on the increase. The ascendancy of property rights in English law may be traced to the reign of Henry VIII, who in the 1530s began appropriating Church and monastic land revenues to the Crown. In stages from 1535 until 1547, the Crown confiscated Church and monastic property.

Henry sold off these lands to courtiers and allies, many of them wealthy merchants and financiers in London. One consequence of these dealings was to sever all the customary rights and feudal relations of the peasants who had lived on the land, hunted in the forests, and grazed their beasts on the common areas. As one of Henry's grantees said to the peasants living on land he had bought from the King:

> Do ye not know that the King's Grace has put down all the houses of monks, friars, and nuns? Therefore, now is the time come that we gentlemen will pull down the houses of such poor knaves as ye be.

The new owners pushed ahead with their plans to use the

lands, violating even the parliamentary restrictions on converting common land to pasture. One churchman wrote of how the mythology of Henry's stated purpose was belied by events:

> In suppressing of abbies, cloisters, colleges, and chantries, the intent of the King's Majesty that dead is, was, and of this our King now is, very godly, and the purpose, or else the pretence, of other wondrous goodly: that thereby such abundance of goods as was superstitiously spent upon vain ceremonies, or voluptuously upon idle bellies, might come to the King's hands to bear his great charges, necessarily bestowed on the common wealth, or partly unto other men's hands, for the better relief of the poor, the maintenance of learning, and the setting forth of God's word. Howbeit, covetous officers have so used this matter, that even those goods which did serve to the relief of the poor, the maintenance of learning, and to comfortable necessity hospitality in the common wealth, be now turned to maintain worldly, wicked, covetous ambition. . . . You which have gotten these goods into your own hands, to turn them from evil to worse, and other goods more from good unto evil, be ye sure that it is even you that have offended God, beguiled the king, robbed the rich, spoiled the poor, and brought a common wealth into a common misery.[68]

Here again is a romantic mythological vision of feudal and ecclesiastical generosity toward the peasantry, mixed with a truth about the erosion of peasant customary rights.

The Evanescence of Custom

The fate of customary rights to till and graze animals on common land traced a path later followed by the right to pass out handbills on the street, and (as a following essay shows) the long-held notion that the broadcast airwaves somehow belong to the people generally.[69] In early eighteenth-century England, Parliament passed the Black Act, which

> defined about one hundred separate felonies, all punishable by hanging. These included arson, blackmail, and forms of mob violence. For our purposes, the most interesting part of this extraordinarily savage legislation is that it made felonious the taking of rabbits from a warren, fish from a pond, or deer from a forest, as well as the cutting of any tree. To be sure, the taking or cutting had to occur in an enclosed park, garden, or forest; but the Crown and the wealthy gentry owned most of the enclosed land. The livelihood of the Hampshire peasantry depended upon access to things that abounded in the wild state: deer, fish, and rabbits to eat, and wood for burning and building. The Black Act and its extremely harsh enforcement essentially criminalized a peasant way of life.[70]

In 1842, the Rhine Provincial Assembly in Germany decreed that gathering fallen wood was to be treated, and punished, as theft. Peasants had been accustomed to gather fallen wood for heating and cooking. By the simple application of the property norm, "gathering" became "pilfering." Karl Marx, then twenty-four years old and having earned his PhD the year before, wrote a series of articles about the legislation:

But whereas these customary rights of the aristoc-
racy are customs which are contrary to the concep-
tion of rational right, the customary rights of the
poor are rights which are contrary to the customs of
positive law. . . . Little thought is needed to perceive
how one-sidedly enlightened legislation has treated
and been compelled to treat the customary rights of
the poor. . . .

In regard to civil law, the most liberal legislations have been confined to formulating and raising
to a universal level those rights which they found already in existence. Where they did not find any such
rights, neither did they create any. They abolished
particular customs, but in so doing forgot that whereas the wrong of the estates took the form of arbitrary
pretensions, the right of those without social estates
appeared in the form of accidental concessions. . . .

These legislations were necessarily one-sided, for
all customary rights of the poor were based on the
fact that certain forms of property were indeterminate in character, for they were not definitely private
property, but neither were they definitely common
property, being a mixture of private and public right,
such as we find in all the institutions of the Middle
Ages. Understanding therefore abolished the hybrid,
indeterminate forms of property by applying to
them the existing categories of abstract ... law.

SLAPP-HAPPY: FRIES WITH THAT

In 1986, a small London organization devoted to environ-
mental protection published a pamphlet attacking McDonald's. The pamphlet, written by Helen Steel and David Mor-

ris, said that McDonald's seeks to deny its workers the right to join labor unions, underpays its workers, causes environmental and social harm in Third World countries by its purchasing practices, sells unhealthy food, and uses misleading advertising. McDonald's reacted by hiring investigators to infiltrate the organization, steal documents, and gather evidence. McDonald's sued Ms. Steel and Mr. Morris for libel. McDonald's offered several times to dismiss its lawsuit if the pamphlet's authors would "stop criticizing McDonald's." The authors declined the offer.

Eventually, McDonald's won a libel judgment against Ms. Steel and Mr. Morris for £40,000. In turn, Ms. Steel and Mr. Morris sued Scotland Yard for having unlawfully provided private information to McDonald's and won £10,000. Throughout the litigation, Ms. Steel and Mr. Morris acted as their own counsel, sometimes with the assistance of a volunteer law student.

Ms. Steel and Mr. Morris took their case to the European Court of Human Rights in Strasbourg. They filed a claim against the United Kingdom, alleging that the UK laws on libel, as applied to them, violated the European Convention on Human Rights provisions on freedom of expression. The ECHR issued its judgment on February 15, 2005, holding that the UK courts had violated Article 6 of the European Convention on Human Rights by not giving Steel and Morris a fair trial, and that their conduct was protected by the European Convention. The Court awarded Ms. Steel and Mr. Morris £24,000 in damages, plus their costs of litigation, that sum to be paid by the UK government.

The McDonald's libel suit was a Strategic Lawsuit Against Public Participation—a SLAPP.[71] During the 1980s and 1990s, corporations filed more than 2,000 SLAPP suits against public interest organizations and their members. The corporations lost almost all of these lawsuits. The suits followed a familiar pattern, alleging that the defendants had libeled the corporation and its products and activities, and that the defendants were committing extortion by trying to force the corporation to change its ways.

The fact that a corporation would almost surely lose a SLAPP suit was not much of a deterrent. Under American law, the general rule is that the losing party in civil litigation need not pay the opponent's legal fees. As these cases dragged on, sometimes for years, the legal fees and costs mounted. The purpose of SLAPP suits was, therefore, not so much to win damages, but to use the threat of damages and the cost of litigation to chill the exercise of protected rights. As one judge in the New York courts remarked, "Short of a gun to the head, a greater threat to First Amendment expression can scarcely be imagined." One is reminded again of Learned Hand's remark: "I must say that, as a litigant, I should dread a lawsuit beyond almost anything short of sickness and death." Indeed, because a SLAPP suit may itself be characterized as a form of extortion, or at least an interference with protected rights of expression, defendants in such suits have brought counterclaims against the corporation that has sought to silence their protests.

Several state legislatures passed laws restricting SLAPP suits and providing that the defendant could recover attorney fees and costs. State courts recognized that the right to petition—such as through community campaigns targeting corporate wrongdoing—exists alongside the right to participate in public debate in other ways. There are national and local organizations devoted to helping defendants in SLAPP suits and to seeking law reform to limit the use of such suits.

A Lawsuit Lovely as a Tree

In 2013, Resolute Forest Products, a conglomerate engaged in logging and the production of forest products, filed a $300 million lawsuit against Greenpeace, affiliated organizations, and Greenpeace leaders. Resolute alleged that Greenpeace itself was a fraud, and that the defendants had committed fraud, extortion, conspiracy, libel, and unlawful interference with business relations. Resolute is based in Canada, but it filed the lawsuit in Atlanta, Georgia. This was not Resolute's first suit against Greenpeace. Other cases, filed in Canada, had been dismissed. The Atlanta case was brought by Donald Trump's favorite New York law firm.

Resolute's 190-page complaint alleged that Greenpeace had falsely portrayed the company as an irresponsible destroyer of prime forest lands covering more than a quarter of Canada's territory, and in the process doing harm to lands on which Native Americans[72] pursued their lives and sustenance, and destroying wildlife habitat. The complaint begins:

> "Greenpeace" is a global fraud. For years, this international network of environmental groups collectively calling themselves "Greenpeace" has fraudulently induced people throughout the United States and the world to donate millions of dollars based on materially false and misleading claims about its purported environmental purpose and its "campaigns" against targeted companies. Maximizing donations, not saving the environment, is Greenpeace's true objective. Consequently, its campaigns are consistently based on sensational misinformation untethered to facts or science, but crafted instead to induce strong emotions and, thereby, donations. Moreover, virtually all

of Greenpeace's fraudulently induced donations are used to perpetuate the corrupted entity itself and the salaries of its leaders and employees.

. . . . .

Beyond direct donations, Greenpeace's lies generate support for boycotts and other adverse actions against its targets and those who dare do business with them. Greenpeace uses these boycotts and other attacks, and the threat of them, to extort public concessions, endorsements, and other benefits from its targets, which it then promotes to potential donors as successes or other reasons to provide even further financial support.

For nineteen numbered paragraphs, the complaint sketches an image of Greenpeace as a powerful collection of fraudsters, lining their pockets by falsely claiming that corporations and governments are harming the environment. Only then does Resolute turn to making specific claims of wrongdoing.

One could characterize this lawsuit in many ways. At bottom, Resolute seeks to defend its property-based right to profit from logging lands, most of which are in some sense "public," and on which Native Americans and others exercised custom-based rights, and on which animals were simply living.

The federal court in Atlanta noted that Resolute did almost no business in Georgia, and that Greenpeace's activity there was fairly minimal. That court transferred the case to the United States District Court for the Northern District of California in San Francisco, reasoning that some relevant part of Greenpeace's alleged conduct took place in California.

The California federal judge dismissed the lawsuit. At bottom, the judge held, this was a SLAPP, devised to deter and punish free expression and organization around environ-mental and human rights issues.[73] Resolute is, the court said, a public figure. Its complaint did not make a plausible claim that any statements by or on behalf of Greenpeace were made with knowledge they were false or with reckless disregard for truth. Indeed, most of Greenpeace's alleged statements were not "factual" at all, but rather expressions of opinion, which the First Amendment absolutely protects. Many of the state-ments were based on reliable scientific research.

As for fraud and extortion, the court noted that Resolute did not claim to have been the victim of any such thing. It had never made a donation to Greenpeace, whether in reliance on Greenpeace's statements or otherwise. As the judge said:

> [E]ven if Greenpeace sought to harm Resolute through Resolute's customers, it did not seek to obtain the business assets it sought to deprive Resolute of. Any alleged property transfer induced by fraud, co-ercion, or threats, moved between Greenpeace and its donors, or between Resolute and its customers. There was no alleged property transfer between Greenpeace and Resolute.[74]

Because the judge found that the anti-SLAPP law of Cali-fornia applied, Resolute was liable for attorney fees and costs.

It is a measure of corporate power that the lengthy dismissal opinion did not deter Resolute. The judge was required to give Resolute an opportunity to file an amended complaint, seeking to correct the defect the court had detect-ed. And so, twenty-three days after the order of dismissal, Resolute filed an amended complaint, with the same intro-ductory nineteen-paragraph farrago of myth and exaggera-tion. The matter is pending as this book goes to press.

Radio Days: The Property Norm Devours the
Mythology of Free Expression

In 1964, a Pennsylvania radio station owned by Red Lion Corporation broadcast a speech by the Reverend Billy James Hargis, who attacked the investigative journalist Fred J. Cook. He claimed that Cook's biography of Senator Barry Goldwater was "a smear," and that Cook had associated with Communists, supported Communist causes, and smeared the FBI. Hargis was a right-wing evangelist preacher who occupied much media attention in the 1950s, 1960s, and 1970s. He founded a college in Oklahoma, and sponsored hospitals, clinics, and missionary centers. His star faded when the IRS investigated the finances of his ecclesiastical empire, and it dimmed even more when male and female congregants accused him of sexual misconduct. One such couple—a male and a female—said he had sex with both of them on their wedding night. (It is not known if they each got equal time.) Hargis admitted to having sex with men and said he had been influenced in doing so by passages in the Bible. He was a colorful speaker: in a verbal attack on Cuba, he referred to "Fido Castro, Khrushchev's little puppy dog."

Cook was a celebrated writer whose work on the FBI and the surveillance state continues to command attention. Having heard of the broadcast, Cook demanded that the station broadcast a rebuttal. At that time, the FCC enforced the "fairness doctrine." The doctrine required that broadcasters serve the public by airing all sides of public issues, and giving persons subjected to personal attack on the airwaves a right of reply. A separate part of federal law required that political candidates be given equal time; this provision did not apply to advertising time the candidate purchased.

Red Lion refused Cook's request. The FCC held that

Cook had a right of reply. Red Lion sought judicial review of this decision, first in the United States Court of Appeals for the D.C. Circuit and then, after the D.C. Circuit upheld the FCC's position, in the Supreme Court. The Supreme Court upheld the fairness doctrine, the origins and purpose of which it described as follows:

> Before 1927, the allocation of [the limited spectrum of broadcast] frequencies was left entirely to the private sector, and the result was chaos. It quickly became apparent that broadcast frequencies constituted a scarce resource whose use could be regulated and rationalized only by the Government. Without government control, the medium would be of little use because of the cacophony of competing voices, none of which could be clearly and predictably heard. Consequently, the Federal Radio Commission was established to allocate frequencies among competing applicants in a manner responsive to the public "convenience, interest, or necessity." [75]

The fairness doctrine was therefore the logical result of the inherent limits of the broadcast spectrum. Moreover, the spectrum is just "there," like sunlight; it cannot rationally be said to belong to anybody. The U.S. regulatory apparatus was part of an international effort that allocated access among countries and for various purposes, of which radio broadcasting was only one.

There is an analogy here to the allocation of common land for pasturage in an earlier time, and to governmental regulation of access to streets and parks and other public spaces that are suitable venues for free expression. In the latter instance, the First Amendment has been thought to require that a public resource be available, and that decisions about utilization be content-neutral and not subject to the unbridled discretion of public officials.

The decline and demise of the fairness doctrine traces a path that reminds one of shopping malls, and even of monasteries: the rights to speak and hear, rooted in principles of free expression, yield to the property norm. The consequent suppression of speech is heralded as a triumph of freedom.

Red Lion was decided in 1969, just one year after the *Logan Valley* case had upheld the right to picket at a Pennsylvania shopping mall. *Red Lion* did not speak of a constitutional entitlement to expression. The Court held only that under a sensible view of the Communications Act, and in accord with evident congressional purpose, the FCC's imposition of the fairness doctrine was reasonable.

Broadcasters continued to pressure the FCC to abandon the fairness doctrine. In 1987, with the support of the Reagan administration, they won.[76] Their theory was that if one built a radio or television station, and obtained a license to broadcast, compelling the station owner to broadcast particular content infringed on the owner's First Amendment rights. This theory may be restated as follows: just as a private shopping mall owner may control the messages and messengers who will engage in free expression on "its" premises, so the broadcaster may control access to its broadcasting equipment. And, just as it violates the First Amendment to compel anyone to speak a particular message, compelling the broadcaster to carry opposing points of view is likewise forbidden by the Constitution.

Mythology upon mythology: First, invoking the property norm is factitious—it costs a lot to build and equip a radio station, but the value of that property is negligible without access to the public space known as the airwaves. Second, given that the spectrum is a common good, the property right of the station owner must logically be mediated by the free expression rights of communicators, to foster the purposes of free expression.

As the state departed the marketplace, it left the field open for monopolization. The innovations of telephone, radio, television, audio recording, video recording, and the expanded means of communication, enabled communication to reach an ever broader audience, and provided greater and greater opportunities for expression. These opportunities were decisively undermined by the concentration of media ownership. *Monthly Review* and its authors have traced these developments.[77] As noted above, Justice Louis Brandeis wrote, in a 1927 criminal syndicalism case:

> If there be time to expose through discussion the falsehood and fallacies, to avert the evil by the process of education, the remedy to be applied is more speech, not enforced silence. [78]

He was speaking of silence enforced by state repression. The exercise of monopoly power proves to be as potent an enforcer.

As Seen on TV

Until I was eleven, we had a big Zenith radio in the living room. After school and my paper route deliveries, I listened to Bobby Benson of the B-Bar-B, *Sky King*, *Roy Rogers*, and *Straight Arrow*. I lobbied my mom to buy the sponsors' products. *Straight Arrow* wanted you to eat Nabisco Shredded Wheat, and in each box were cards that described alleged Native American crafts. These were called "Injun-uities."

I don't remember which program endorsed the breakfast cereal company from which you could get a decoder ring, for boxtops and a buck.

When the people down the block got a television set, I used to go over to their house and watch. I liked the dramatic program *Medic*, starring Richard Boone. Thinking to shock my grandmother, in whose house we lived and who took us every Sunday to the Lake Street Baptist Church, I came home one day and reported, "Grandma, next week on *Medic* they are going to circumcise Charlie McCarthy." She looked up from her newspaper and said, "What are they going to use, dear, a pencil sharpener?"

When I was seventeen, I went to work for a nonprofit, non-commercial radio station in Berkeley. By that time, I had a pretty good idea of how broadcast outlets paid their bills. Outside the little nascent community that was to become "public radio" and "public television," what we hear and see was determined by the owners of broadcast stations, and by those who paid to have content broadcast.

In 2002, Congress passed the Bipartisan Campaign Reform Act.[79] The act prohibited corporations from using their general treasury funds to pay for "electioneering communication" or for communications that expressly advocate the election or defeat of a candidate. An electioneering communication was "any broadcast, cable, or satellite communication" that "refers to a clearly identified candidate for Federal office" and is made within 30 days of a primary election . . . and that was "publicly distributed." In the case of a candidate for nomination for President, electioneering communication was one that could "be received by 50,000 or more persons in a State where a primary election . . . is being held within 30 days."

In 2010, in *Citizens United v. Federal Election Commis-*

sion,[80] the Supreme Court held, 5 to 4, that most of the BPCR violated the First Amendment. The central holding was that corporations have the First Amendment right of free speech. The practical consequence of this ruling is that we are deluged with political communications paid for by corporations who support reactionary politicians: Money is speech. Voices will be heard in the electronic marketplace just to the extent that they can pay the admission fee.

The Court imagined for us a world in which all the potential buyers of broadcast time operate on a basis of formal equality. The individual with a net worth of $50,000 stands as "equal" to a multibillion-dollar multinational—both have the same equal right to have their message broadcast. This mythological equality surpasses Anatole France's observation about the individual rich person and the individual poor person having the equal right to beg in the streets.

A "corporation" is a capital-pooling device, permitting many capitals to be united and thus to exercise greater power in the marketplace. This inanimate form has existed in various forms for millennia, but it had become the dominant form of industrial capital by the mid-nineteenth century. The legal rights and duties of this "juridical person" have been the subject of great debate. Baron Thurlow, an eighteenth-century Lord Chancellor of England, is reported to have exclaimed, "Did you ever expect a corporation to have a conscience, when it has no soul to be damned, and no body to be kicked?" One report has him adding, "And, by God, it ought to have both."[81]

In 1909, the New York Central Railroad, a corporation, was charged with a crime because one of its agents, acting with the intent to benefit the corporation, paid illegal rebates to shippers. Under the Elkins Act, this was an unlawful interference with free competition. New York Central argued that finding the corporation guilty would harm the individual shareholders, thus depriving them of property without having an opportunity to be heard. The Supreme Court rejected this argument, recognizing that a corporation's ability to wreak harm could lawfully be restrained:

> Since a corporation acts by its officers and agents their purposes, motives, and intent are just as much those of the corporation as are the things done. If, for example, the invisible, intangible essence of air, which we term a corporation, can level mountains, fill up valleys, lay down iron tracks, and run railroad cars on them, it can intend to do it, and can act therein as well viciously as virtuously.[82]

New York Central contains at least a glimmer of recognition that a corporation has power that surpasses that of any human person. That glimmer did not illuminate the *Citizens United* decision.

THE PENTAGON PAPERS: PRIVATIZING JOHN ADAMS'S "GENERAL KNOWLEDGE"

In 1967, Defense Secretary Robert McNamara commissioned a study of the origins and conduct of the Vietnam War. The study was finished on January 15, 1969, five days before Richard Nixon was inaugurated as president. In 47 volumes, consisting of 3,000 pages of analysis and 4,000 pages of government documents, the study chronicled the failures, falsehoods, and illegalities of the war.

Daniel Ellsberg is a Harvard-educated economist. He served in the Marine Corps in Vietnam. During the 1960s, he worked in the Defense Department for a time, and for the

RAND Corporation.[83] While at RAND, he contributed to the Vietnam War study. Ellsberg believed that the study should be made public, to inform and enhance public debate about the war. In October 1969, he made a copy of it.

In March 1971, Ellsberg gave copies of 43 of the 47 volumes to a *New York Times* reporter. In June, he gave copies to a *Washington Post* reporter. The "Pentagon Papers" controversy began. The Nixon administration sued to prevent publication. The case quickly reached the Supreme Court. The Court held, 6–3, that preventing publication would be an unconstitutional prior restraint on press freedom. In the meantime, Alaska Senator Gravel had put most of the Papers' content into the *Congressional Record*; he was immunized from reprisals by the "Speech or Debate" clause of the Constitution.[84]

Ellsberg and his colleague Daniel Russo were indicted for their role in releasing the Papers. The indictment contained a foreseeable collection of charges centering on alleged harm to the national defense. But in its verbiage lurked a rather dramatic claim about property. Ellsberg and Russo were charged with "steal[ing]" or "purloin[ing]" a "thing of value" belonging to the United States. That is, their making and keeping a copy of documents, the originals of which remained in the government's possession, was theft of the *information* in the documents. The government thus claimed that virtually all the information in its possession was a form of property, to which it laid claim in opposition to any citizen claim of a customary or other right of access to knowledge about his or her government.

Information may be property under some circumstances. The Constitution gives Congress the power:

To promote the Progress of Science and useful Arts, by

securing for limited Times to Authors and Inventors the exclusive Right to their respective Writings and Discoveries.

This right of property, through patents and copyright, is accorded only for a "limited time," and on condition that the work be publicly disclosed. The Framers of the Constitution did not provide that government would have a property right in writings it created. In England, there is "Crown Copyright." The United States does not have such a thing, perhaps because of Madison's assurance that we reject "the impious doctrine of the Old World that people were made for Kings and not Kings for people."[85] United States law provides that "copyright protection under this title is not available for any work of the United States government."[86]

John Adams had spoken of the "undisputable, unalienable, indefeasible divine right to the most dreaded and most envied kind of knowledge, I mean of the characters and conduct of their rulers." It turns out that this is just another custom-based entitlement.

By characterizing all "its" information as property, the law of theft immediately reaches the whistleblower who reveals agency misconduct, without any troubling need to show that there are real state secrets—or even such things as privacy concerns—at stake. Government thus derives all the benefits of a robust law of state secrets, without the burden of showing that any particular item of information merits secrecy.

We had perhaps believed that the information held by our government was our common patrimony. Not so. The property norm vests title in the state, effectively accomplishing the same thing as a wholesale invocation of secrecy.

Hans Magnus Enzensberger has written:

State secret and espionage as legal concepts are inventions of the late nineteenth century. They were born out of the spirit of imperialism. Their victorious march begins in 1894 with the Dreyfus affair. The mana of the state secret communicates itself to its bearers and immunizes them, each according to the degree of his initiation, against the question; therefore they are free not to answer and, in the real sense of the word, are irresponsible. How many state secrets someone knows becomes the measure of his rank and his privilege in a finely articulated hierarchy. The mass of the governed is without secrets; that is, it has no right to partake of power, to criticize it and watch over it. [87]

The presiding judge dismissed the Ellsberg-Russo case when it became apparent that the Nixon administration had committed burglary and conducted illegal electronic surveillance in order to gather evidence, and had tried to suborn the judge by offering him a position as FBI director. However, the "theft" theory reappeared in other cases involving disclosure of information about the working of government.

Government monopolization of information is mirrored in the private sector. If a corporation has devised a process from which it intends to profit, if may eschew the public disclosure required by seeking a patent or copyrighting information. It calls the information a "trade secret" and takes steps to keep it secret.[88]

—— 4 ——

Mythologies of Worker Rights

WHO IS INTIMIDATING WHOM?

SMITHFIELD FOODS, BASED IN the eponymous North Carolina city, packages pork and poultry products. Through mergers and acquisitions, it had by 2008 become the largest pork and turkey processing company in the world, with annual revenues of 12 billion dollars. Its workers were not represented by a union. The United Food and Commercial Workers Union began to organize Smithfield workers under the provisions of the National Labor Relations Act. Two-thirds of Smithfield's workers were African American, living in the American South and working for low wages. Many other workers were immigrants.

Smithfield retaliated. It reported immigrant workers who were union supporters to the federal immigration authorities, so that the workers would be deported. It fired other union supporters. Smithfield harassed union sympathizers. All the while, working conditions at the plant were unsafe while workers labored for low wages. The union filed administrative complaints under federal labor law, but these did not succeed in forcing extensive changes. Smithfield management feared that if workers at its core facility in North Carolina were to gain collective bargaining rights, this would lead to unionization campaigns throughout the company.

Finally, faced with Smithfield's well-financed efforts to

derail an old-style organizing drive, the UFCW and its sympathizers embarked on a community campaign. They sought support in the community where the Smithfield factory was located, and in the food service industry generally.

Smithfield responded by suing the UFCW and some of its officers under the federal racketeering statute, known by the acronym RICO.[89] Smithfield claimed that the union engaged in a "pattern of racketeering" by attempting to commit "extortion." The alleged extortion consisted of the union trying to influence people to pressure Smithfield to recognize the union and sign a collective bargaining agreement that would raise worker pay and improve working conditions. Under the RICO statute, Smithfield sought "at least in excess of $5,900,000," tripled under the RICO law, attorney fees, an injunction requiring UFCW to shut down its community campaign, and "other relief."[90]

Extortion? Under English common law, extortion was a misdemeanor that a public official would commit by demanding a fee where none was due, or a larger fee than the law provided. In modern times, most states make it a crime for anyone—public official or not—to demand or seek money or property by threats.[91] Smithfield alleged that some of the threats involved violence, but its main claim was that any organized effort by a group of workers to influence employer conduct is a basis for a lawsuit. Smithfield did not want to part with its money and property by raising wages. It was being forced to do so.

If the workers wanted a union, they should continue to work within the limits of the provably ineffective federal labor law.

For more than three hundred years, employers have been rushing to court, claiming that organized workers are unlawfully trying by conspiracy and coercion to get higher wages, and getting legislatures to pass laws against that sort of thing. One might have thought that in the twenty-first century workers' rights would be so universally recognized that no employer would hire a bunch of very costly lawyers to bring a lawsuit like *Smithfield v. UFCW*.

In the marketplace of pork, Smithfield was under the usual pressures. Competitors said that their pork was better, tastier, less laden with cholesterol, easier to prepare. It was not just "the other white meat," but the best white meat. In the world of mergers and acquisitions, Smithfield no doubt encountered hard bargaining, perhaps having to pay more for an acquisition target than it wanted to. Among all these pressures, how could Smithfield claim that the voices of indignant workers and community leaders were so far from an acceptable social bargaining norm that these voices should be silenced and the speakers compelled to pay damages? And by what reasoning could the theory of such a claim be based on the principle that the speakers were committing a crime?

A federal trial judge upheld Smithfield's legal theory. Despite this initial success in court, Smithfield could not be sure that its position would be sustained on appeal. The community campaign had continued. Late in 2008, Smithfield and the union reached a settlement. The terms of this settlement are secret, having been sealed by the court. According to public news reports, Smithfield withdrew its RICO allegations. There has been a successful union election at Smithfield. From the available public evidence, therefore, the RICO strategy did not achieve success in the sense of a judicial victory. It did, however, force the union into an expensive court battle.

The question remains: How did the extortion mythology, with its skewed sense of what is and is not a free bargain, arise?

CONTRACT, CONSPIRACY, AND WORKER CONSENT

With the right of property established as a relationship between people and things—from at least the 1600s
onward—people without property worked for people whose
property consisted of means of production. The contract of
labor was, so the mythology of social relations had it, a free
bargain. Karl Renner wrote of this contract:

> The fiction of free choice masks the reality that the
> wage-laborer's lack of property compels him to hire
> out at wage-work. To put it another way, the notion
> that property is no more than a relationship between
> a person (*persona*) and a thing (*res*), and therefore in-
> volves no domination of person over person, is a fic-
> tion. Control of property—when property consists of
> means of production—is converted into control over
> persons through the medium of the contract to work;
> thus the idea of contract as free bargain is itself ren-
> dered illusory. [92]

The worker needs a wage. He can work for what the
employer offers or try to find a job someplace else. To increase
their bargaining power, workers formed associations. These
groups vowed to withhold the labor of all the members
unless wages and working conditions were improved. Members had to agree not to work except on terms negotiated by
the association.

Employers turned to the law. The right of every worker
to withhold his consent to low wages was part of capitalism's
mythology, but it was an *individual* right. If a group of workers used it as a *social* right, the state charged that they had

sought to achieve their lawful goal of raising wages by an unlawful means. That was conspiracy in restraint of trade.

Here is a case report from 1721, in London:

> One Wise and several other journeymen tailors, of or in the town of Cambridge, were indicted for a conspiracy amongst themselves to raise their wages, and were found guilty.
>
>   The Court. The indictment, it is true, sets forth that the defendants refused to work under the wages which they demanded; . . . yet it is not for the refusing to work, but for conspiring that they are indicted, and a conspiracy of any kind is illegal, although the matter about which they conspired might have been lawful for them, or any of them to do, if they had not conspired to do it. [93]

The revolutionary movements that had swept feudalism away were designed to uphold individual liberty and not social justice. The right to bargain for conditions of work, free from feudal exactions, evaporated as soon as workers organized in order to have more bargaining power.

In Philadelphia, in the 1820s, an employer in the garment trade expanded his business along Chestnut Street so that he could effectively control the wages of journeymen tailors. The tailors organized and were convicted of conspiracy. Their lawyer, David Paul Brown, noted the contradictions of the prosecutor's theory:

> Combinations of this sort are more dangerous in masters than in men, because poverty is a law which man cannot resist. Masters have the means, and though

they may exact from their customers any price which they please, there is never a thought of their being conspirators, while they are grinding down the men whom they employ, to little more than nothing, and pocketing their services.

Judges waved away such arguments, saying it was "no matter what the defendants' motives were, whether to resist the supposed oppression of their masters, or to insist upon extravagant wages." In some states, conspiracy was made a crime by the legislature; in others, it was a judge-made "common law crime."[94]

The conspiracy theory was a myth, elaborated to justify a claim that employers were being coerced to consent to raising wages.[95]

The "conspiracy in restraint of trade" mythology persisted into the twentieth century, as union organizing increased. In 1912, Clarence Darrow summed up the state of things at a public meeting in Portland, Oregon:

When they want a working man for anything excepting work they want him for conspiracy. And the greatest conspiracy that is possible for a working man to be guilty of is not to work—a conspiracy the other fellows are always guilty of. . . . In England, in the early days . . . for one working man to go to another and suggest that he ask for higher wages was a conspiracy, punishable by imprisonment. For a few men to come together and form a labor organization in England was a conspiracy. It is not here. Even the employer is willing to let you form labor organizations, if you don't do anything but pass resolutions.[96]

Darrow then turned to the Sherman Antitrust Act of 1890, a statute designed to curb the monopolization of rail, petroleum, mining, steel, and other industries. The trouble was that the drafters of the Act, searching around for statutory language, seized upon the common law formulation of "conspiracy in restraint of trade." Those words had a Pavlovian effect on monopolists and their lawyers—and soon on judges.

In 1894, workers at the Pullman Company went on strike to protest wage reduction, and conditions of work and life in the company town of Pullman, near Chicago. Under the leadership of Eugene Debs and the American Railway Union, the strike gained worker support until about 250,000 workers were either on strike or were boycotting trains carrying a Pullman car. Rail service in twenty-seven states west of Detroit was halted.

The railroad lawyers sued the union and its leaders in federal court under the Sherman Act, for "conspiracy in restraint of trade" and obtained an injunction. Debs was accused of violating the injunction, and held in contempt The case went to the Supreme Court,[97] where the folks who had given us *Plessy v. Ferguson* affirmed Debs's conviction. Thus, a law designed to curb monopoly became monopoly's best friend, and all in the name of free contract. Darrow commented:

> The [Sherman Act] was debated long in Congress and the Senate. Every man spoke of it as a law against the trusts and monopolies, conspiracies in restraint of trade and commerce. Every newspaper in the country discussed it as that; every labor organization so considered it. Congress passed it and the President signed it, and then an indictment was found against

a corporation, and it went to the Supreme Court of the United States for the Supreme Court to say what the law meant. . . . And after awhile there came along the strike of a body of laboring men, the American Railway Union. They didn't have a dollar in the world altogether, because they were laboring men and they were not engaged in trade; they were working; but they hadn't found anything else that the Sherman Antitrust Act applied to, so they indicted Debs and his followers for a conspiracy in restraint of trade; and they carried this case to the Supreme Court. I was one of the attorneys who carried it to the Supreme Court. Most lawyers only tell you about the cases they win. I can tell you about some I lose. A lawyer who wins all his cases does not have many.

President Grover Cleveland called in the Army and the U.S. Marshal Service to break up the strike, city by city.

And so it went. During the 1920s, there were more than a thousand judicial orders forbidding workers from striking and otherwise impeding labor organizational efforts. Employers routinely forced workers to sign a contract agreeing that they would not join a labor union. At the same time, employers' organizations imposed discipline on any member who agreed to negotiate with a union.

In 1932, Congress passed the Norris-LaGuardia Act, which prohibited federal courts from issuing orders that prevented peaceful labor organizing and outlawed contracts that forced workers to refrain from joining a union. The Wagner Act came along in 1935. It established a National Labor Relations Board, which regulated unionization and provided that if a majority of workers in a particular workplace, who did the same kind of work, voted to be represented by a labor union, the Board would then certify the union as the workers' agent to bargain with the employer about wages and working conditions.

The Norris-LaGuardia and Wagner Acts ended the use of conspiracy in restraint of trade as capital's weapon against workers. The RICO suits against community organizing campaigns seek to keep the old mythology alive. The form of words is different, but underneath is this enduring image of the individual worker and the monopolistic enterprise, standing as social equals, and the worker being told not to disturb this imagined balance by ganging up with others.

THE NINETEENTH-CENTURY WORKER IN THE COURTS

In the nineteenth century, worker unity was a restraint of trade. Therefore, the ordinary rules of free market contract applied to workers and employers. So, too, did the ordinary rules of tort, that is, liability for civil damages.

Professor Wythe Holt has chronicled nineteenth-century cases of workers who signed on for a term of weeks or months at a fixed remuneration, and who for one reason or another quit before the term was up. The courts denied them any pay for the time that they had worked. A contract is a contract, and must be fulfilled faithfully, said the judges. If the worker argued that contracts are based on mutual consent, the courts replied that a bargain is a bargain even if the worker did not understand it. Here, then, is another theme in the mythology of consent. Given the expansion of commerce and industry, many workers hardly spoke English, so consent to their supposed bargain was even more attenuated.

The worker who entered employment in public works and manufacture faced dangerous working conditions.[98] One thousand workers died during construction of the Erie

Canal. At least 1,200 died building the Transcontinental Rail-road that was completed in 1869; most of these were Chinese immigrants. In the eastern United States, many if not most of the railroad workers were Irish immigrants; even today, research continues to locate the gravesites where sometimes dozens of them were buried.

The injured worker, or the family of a dead worker, might seek damages from the employer, only to run into barriers to achieving justice. If the employer's negligence caused death or injury, then in theory the employer would be liable in damages. The operative words are "in theory." The employee had to find a lawyer willing to take the case. Bar association rules discouraged lawyers from working on a contingent fee basis and prohibited lawyers from seeking out injured clients. Later, labor unions helped steer workers to lawyers who would help them, but bar associations attacked such arrangements until finally, in 1964, the Supreme Court held that workers and their union had the right to work together to provide counsel.[99]

In court, the employee faced the triple threat of employ-er defenses: contributory negligence, the fellow servant rule, and assumption of the risk. These three defenses flourished well into the twentieth century. They were abolished by federal law in 1908 for injured railroad workers but stuck around for decades in most other fields.[100] The rules were devised and elaborated by courts as part of a pattern of judi-cial decisions designed to favor the interests of industrial and mercantile capital.

If the employee's injury or death was caused, even in part, by his own negligence, then he was barred from recovery.

If the injury or death was caused by the negligence of a fellow worker, the worker's recovery was reduced or elim-inated. The "fellow servant" rule came into United States law from England in 1842.[101] A train derailed because an employee at the depot failed to throw a switch. The train engineer is injured. Under ordinary principles, the switchman's negligence would be chargeable to the railroad. But the engineer was an employee of the same railroad company, a "fellow servant." The Massachusetts court invoked the theory of free bargain, and denied the engineer's claim. When one accepts employment, the court held, one is presumed to agree to the risk that one's fellow employees may act carelessly.

So here is the market-based rule: employees in the same occupation are forbidden to band together to enforce adequate wages and working conditions. Those in a particular trade may not collectively demand that only members of their organization be hired, even though one purpose of such an arrangement is often to insist that the members have certain qualifications. Put another way, the workers could not gather to discuss working conditions, but were bound together by a rule that made them all responsible for one another's conduct.

The theory behind assumption of the risk was similarly mythological. One who chose to be employed in a dangerous workplace had to accept the consequences. "Chose"? Waves of Irish immigrants fled famine, poverty, and English agricultural policies that undermined peasant life and livelihood. Chinese immigrants who built the railroad had been rounded up by labor contractors.

Not all judicial incarnations of the triple threat anti-worker rules gave the employer a victory. In the mid-twentieth century, an oil rig worker named Billy slipped and fell, suffering serious injury. At trial, the employer proved that there had been a pile of oily rags on the drilling platform, and that Billy had passed by that pile of rags more than a dozen times and could not have missed seeing it. The judge, as requested by the employer, instructed the jurors that they must return a verdict for the employer if Billy "knew and appreciated the risk" posed by the rags.

The jurors returned a verdict in Billy's favor, assessing substantial damages. The employer's counsel was surprised. He asked the jury foreman how such a thing was possible. "Well," said the foreman, "we just followed the judge's instructions. Billy knew them rags were there, but he sure as hell did not appreciate it."

There is a mythology of the universality of language; believers in it will run into trouble sooner or later.

SHAKESPEARE ON WORKER CONSENT

In *Henry VI, Part 2*, we read:

> **DICK:** The first thing we do, let's kill all the lawyers.
> **JACK CADE:** Nay, that I mean to do. Is not this a lamentable thing, that of the skin of an innocent lamb should be made parchment? That parchment, being scribbled o'er, should undo a man? Some say the bee stings; but I say, 'tis the bee's wax; for I did but seal once to a thing, and I was never mine own man since.

Shakespeare is giving us a fragment about Jack Cade's rebellion, a peasant uprising in 1450. One grievance of the peasantry, from 1300 onward, was based on an institution known as copyhold. The feudal lord's steward—a sort of lawyer—would draft an instrument on parchment, binding the peasant and his family to work the land and to give over the greater part of what they produced. The parchment, once the peasant had affixed his mark to it on a wax seal, became part of the manorial records. Rebellious peasants were wont to burn the records and hang the steward.

As portrayed by Shakespeare, Cade denounces the living and working conditions he is compelled to endure, and notes that to these impositions is added the indignity of the lord's claim that he has agreed by the "bargain" of copyhold to endure them.

SMITHFIELD REDUX: COMMUNITY ORGANIZING AND EMPLOYER CONSENT

Farm workers and workers who labor in their employers' homes are largely excluded even from meager federal labor law protection, and they have the greatest difficulty in organizing and being heard. In manufacturing industries, employers often respond to worker demands by moving manufacturing operations overseas. That pair of tennis shoes that cost $120 contains labor for which the manufacturer paid $1.20 in Vietnam.

But, when the hotel or hospital sheets are dirty, it is inefficient to send them to a low-wage country and have them shipped back when laundered. So employers created low-wage zones closer to home: they turned to "outsourcing." A hospital in Los Angeles had laundry rooms, where workers laundered the sheets, towels, and uniforms. Workers had fair wages and benefits. To cut costs, the hospital administration made a contract to send all the laundry to a central facility that had similar contracts with hospitals and hotels. In these facilities, wages and working conditions were substandard, and employees were subject to the same kinds of pressures that the Smithfield workers faced.

To reach excluded and scattered workers, the Service Employees International Union (SEIU), the Teamsters

Union, and the United Farm Workers formed an alliance called Change to Win to initiate and support community campaigns.

In 2008, Cintas, a multinational corporation that provides work clothing, laundry, and cleaning services to business and individual customers throughout North America, filed a RICO suit in the federal court in New York. Cintas claimed that the community campaign conducted by the Teamsters and its Change to Win allies amounted to extortion. Cintas also named dozens of individual union organizers and members as defendants.

Cintas employees worked at widely scattered locations, and many employees' patterns of work consisted of moving from site to site to deliver clothing and perform other services. The union had demanded that Cintas accept collective bargaining provided that a majority of the employees signed cards affirming their desire to have a union. When Cintas refused, the union and its allies conducted a public campaign criticizing Cintas for paying "poverty-level" wages, committing violations of the law, and engaging in racial and ethnic discrimination. The union maintained an internet website, telling the public about other uniform suppliers whose workforces were represented in collective bargaining agreements. All of this, the Cintas lawsuit claimed, amounted to extortion.

In March 2009, a federal district judge dismissed Cintas's claims. The judge held that the community campaign was an exercise of free speech rights. In December 2009, the court of appeals affirmed the dismissal.[102]

The federal court's opinion dismissing the complaint sets out a number of significant legal principles. First, the court directly addressed, and rebutted, the extortion mythology. Extortion consists of forcing someone to give up money or property without getting anything in return except an end to coercion. The court held that the public campaign could not be classified as extortion because a collective bargaining agreement has potential benefits for both the employer and the union. Such an agreement is not extortionate, but simply the result of "hard bargaining," which often occurs in the marketplace for all goods and services, including labor power.

Second, the court held that the right of free expression protects the public campaign that the union and its allies conducted. Simply put, the court said, "Cintas does not have a right to operate free from any criticism, organized or otherwise." If public criticism leads consumers and others to have an unfavorable opinion of Cintas, the company has no right to complain. Free speech is not only an individual right; it may be exercised socially and collectively.

SICKENING OPPOSITION TO WORKERS' RIGHTS

Prime Healthcare Services owns and manages hospitals. In 2017 it operated forty-five hospitals in fourteen states. It is a bottom-feeder, buying up financially distressed hospitals and making them profitable. Prime Healthcare achieves cost savings by being, in its words, "largely non-union," and aggressively resisting worker efforts to organize for better wages and working conditions. The *Los Angeles Times* reported in 2007 that Prime's management policies resulted in higher than average profits, achieved at the cost of good patient care. According to the *Times*: "When Prime Healthcare Services Inc., takes over a hospital, it typically cancels insurance contracts, allowing the hospital to collect steeply higher reimbursements. It suspends services—such as chemotherapy treatments, mental health care and birthing centers—that patients need but aren't lucrative." In 2005, two former nurses at Desert Valley Hospital won a lawsuit in which they claimed they were fired in retaliation for reporting that hospital management provided inadequate care to save money and that Prime's founder and CEO, Dr. Prem Reddy, often reported to work while under the influence of alcohol. Prime's hospitals have far higher than average rates of patient septicemia.[103] Prime and its management have been the subject of lawsuits about sexual harassment of employees. Prime has been investigated for seeking enhanced Medicare reimbursements based on misdiagnosing patients as having conditions more severe than they actually had.[104]

It should not surprise us that Prime Healthcare has aggressively fought against its workers' right to organize and bargain collectively. Enter Change to Win, the SEIU-Teamsters-Farm Workers coalition, with community campaigns.

Prime responded to the campaigns in two phases. In 2011, it sued Change to Win and Kaiser Foundation Hospitals, a competing hospital chain, in federal court in San Diego. Prime claimed that the pressure from defendants to accept worker rights violated RICO and the federal labor laws. This part of the lawsuit was in the familiar Smithfield-Cintas form. However, Prime also claimed that Kaiser's relatively more union-friendly policies amounted to an unlawful agreement to restrain trade. This antitrust theory was that if, in a given market, one or more major employers accept union organization of their workers, the negotiations and eventual agreements in this process represent an actionable harm to employers who are anti-union. That is, market pressure exerted by the actions of a competitor undermined Prime's "right" to refuse its consent to worker demands.

The district court dismissed Prime's lawsuit, holding that the antitrust laws did not forbid concerted conduct to compel recognition of worker rights. The court of appeals affirmed the dismissal and the Supreme Court denied certiorari.[105]

Prime was undeterred. Using the same law firm, it brought another suit in 2014. This time, it named only SEIU, Change to Win, and a few individuals with leadership roles in those entities. The lawyers filed the lawsuit in San Francisco federal court, which is in a different federal judicial district from San Diego. This second lawsuit focused only on RICO and federal labor law. The San Francisco court recognized that the new lawsuit bore a great resemblance to the old one, and sent the case to San Diego, where it landed with the same judge who had dismissed the first suit. That judge, Gonzalo Curiel, dismissed the case, basically on the same grounds that the Cintas court had used. Prime appealed. The appeal languished in the court of appeals and Prime eventually abandoned it, in 2017.[106]

5

Mythologies of International Human Rights

The *Kiobel* Case: "United States Law . . . Does Not Rule the World"

ON APRIL 17, 2013, IN *Kiobel v. Royal Dutch Petroleum Co.*,[107] the Supreme Court held, 5 to 4, that victims of human rights violations committed by a subsidiary of Shell Oil had no right to sue in federal court in the United States. In the 1990s, in Nigeria's Ogoniland, residents protested the environmental harm being done by a subsidiary of Royal Dutch Shell and its English affiliate during petroleum exploration and production. The Nigerian government reacted by sending armed forces to plunder villages, and raping and killing protesters. The Shell subsidiary encouraged these actions and provided financial and logistical support.

These were crimes against fundamental principles of human rights. The plaintiffs who brought the case reside in the United States. Indeed, they came to the United States, and were granted asylum there, precisely because of the violence committed by the defendants in their homeland. A private person or entity who aids and abets a state actor in wrongful conduct shares the liability. Under U.S. law, this would be true of a Ku Klux member helping a sheriff's deputy brutalize a civil rights worker, and the Supreme Court has so held.[108] The conduct described in the plaintiffs' case amounts to state-sponsored terrorism, and one had thought that all branches of government have a duty to address and remedy it.

The Court's majority opinion was for five justices, although Justice Kennedy's concurrence suggests a possible limiting principle. Even Chief Justice Roberts's opinion for the majority contains a double-edged caveat: some claims that arise in foreign countries can perhaps be heard, but on the other hand some claims that "touch" the United States may not do so with sufficient force. Four justices concurred in the result, and on a different theory than the majority; their votes, plus that of Justice Kennedy, might signal that there is yet an opportunity to fashion a judicial remedy for the kinds of human rights violations at issue in this case.

That said, the majority opinion is a mess. It mixes up subject matter jurisdiction, forum selection, and choice of law. This folly is all in the service of saying that a venerable federal statute is now made nearly useless to serve its intended and laudable purpose. The Alien Tort Claims Act, or ATCA, has been a formidable weapon in the struggle to obtain redress for victims of human rights crimes.[109] ATCA, which was part of the Judiciary Act of 1789, says that the "district courts shall have original jurisdiction of any civil action by an alien for a tort only committed in violation of the law of nations." The Court held that, despite the act's broad language, and despite the fact that violations of "the law of nations" are not constrained by nation-state borders, the statute does not permit a court to hear any lawsuit involving a wrongful act with allegedly minimal impact on the United States.

The Court said that allowing a court to hear and decide such a case might interfere with the executive branch and congressional control over foreign and military policy, and therefore the statute must be presumed not to have extra-territorial application. Besides, Chief Justice Roberts said, "United States law governs domestically but does not rule the world."

Let us pause here and consider that remark, with a few examples, to see its mythological character:

- U.S. drones have killed several thousand people in Pakistan. About 25 percent of those killed were civilians. Attorney-General Holder said in 2013 that those killed by drones had received "due process" because the drone strikes were approved by a White House committee. Thousands more were killed in other countries. The U.S. government position is that the invasion of these sovereign spaces is permissible under international law. The Supreme Court has held that international law is part of U.S. law.[110]

- Thousands of civilians died from U.S.-led bombings in the Middle East and the former Yugoslavia.

- The United States has about 800 military bases in countries around the world and a military presence in 150 countries.[111]

- A person thought to be a terrorist may be arrested in Afghanistan and taken to the U.S. naval base in Guantánamo Bay, where he will be detained, tortured, and perhaps eventually tried by a military tribunal. The power of "United States law" over those people is based on a theory that they could at some future time either be a threat to U.S. territory or are in some sense combatants against U.S. interests.

- The United States has overthrown or conspired to overthrow governments in, to cite a few examples, Iran (1953), Guatemala (1954), the Dominican Republic (1965), Chile

(1973), and Iraq (2003). In 1984, the CIA mined the harbors of Nicaragua, and then refused to participate in the International Court of Justice proceedings that held that U.S. conduct violated international law.[112] It has propped up dictatorial regimes with arms, money, and military assistance. These actions were undertaken to put U.S. power and influence at the service of multinationals operating in those countries. Shell Oil in Nigeria was just another surfer on the wave of imperial domination.

Did the Chief Justice state an unintentional truth, or perhaps indulge in a subtle irony? U.S. law may not rule the world, but U.S. *lawlessness* is making an effort to do so. If U.S. law does not rule the world, it is not for want of trying.

The real vice of the Chief Justice's expression is that it turns the Constitution on its head.[113] Those who wrote the ATCA did not believe that the law of the United States could or would rule the world. However, they did understand and believe that to some great extent "the world" ruled U. S. law. They were conscious of the imperial power being exercised by Spain, Portugal, France, the Netherlands, and England. They wrote this statute, using the words "the law of nations." These words were those that Blackstone—the legal scholar most familiar to lawyers in 1789—used in his Oxford lectures. They echoed the writings of Hugo Grotius and other seventeenth-century writers, who had a broad and historically rooted understanding of the limits on permissible sovereign conduct.

The 1789 authors might have said instead "international law," for that phrase had also come into use around 1776 in an essay by Jeremy Bentham, who credited a French legal writer for first using the word *international*. Bentham sharply rebuked the Blackstone formulation of "law of nations," and argued that there could be no such law that stood any higher than the will of a particular sovereign. That is, if the Spanish wanted to sponsor piracy, or the Portuguese wanted to indulge in torture or the slave trade or any such iniquity, neither the world community nor any other sovereign state had any right to say anything about it.

By choosing the phrase "law of nations," the Congress intended in 1789 to give the courts the power and duty to do what the *Kiobel* Court says they should not do: consider whether the conduct of a foreign person or entity might be subject to suit in the United States courts. Note that I say "might." As we shall see, there are many and sometimes good reasons that such a power should not be exercised in a particular case. But to construe this statute as barring all such exercises is contrary to its text and history.

In addition to ignoring text and history, the Chief Justice's stated rationale also performs a peculiar sleight of hand with respect to constitutional separation of powers. He speaks of deference to foreign policy in the treatment of foreign sovereigns. It is true that the executive branch has great responsibility in that field, and its actions are entitled to deference from the coordinate branches. But in the *Kiobel* case, the government of Nigeria was not a defendant. No foreign sovereign's interest was involved, except perhaps the reputational harm that might be done when the evidence showed that the Nigerian government had colluded with Shell. United States policy toward Nigeria could not possibly be affected by the trial of this lawsuit.

No, the Court accorded the deference due sovereigns to a multinational oil company. Multinationals notoriously seek to avoid accountability by "outsourcing" jobs that can be exported, and by making deals with complicit governments for activities such as agriculture, mining, and oil production that must be done where the goods are grown or found. It is therefore essential that the courts in metropolitan countries where the multinationals have their headquarters take a role in defining and policing illegal conduct. In past times, the Supreme Court has recognized the power of great corporations to do great harm and has wisely interpreted statutes to make them accountable.[114] And we have recently been taught that corporations are persons at least to the extent of having free speech rights.

Sovereigns are amply protected by a broad though not unlimited immunity from suit. Thus, all of the Court's expressed concerns are met by the Foreign Sovereign Immunities Act, under which the *Kiobel* plaintiffs could not have added Nigeria as a defendant.[115] This point simply emphasizes that all the *Kiobel* decision has done is put the mantle of protection normally accorded to sovereigns around the shoulders of Shell Oil.

The doctrine of immunity is powerful. It can and sometimes should be interposed to prevent the courts of one sovereign from imposing their views on another sovereign or its officers. The doctrine has contours and limits that judicial tribunals are busy defining and refining.[116]

Second, a court with subject matter jurisdiction can hold that a lawsuit that arises in a foreign country, and as to which the evidence may be found there, should be tried in that country. That is the doctrine of forum *non conveniens*. Sending a properly filed lawsuit to another country for trial requires detailed consideration of the burdens and benefits of such a change. In striking that balance, courts typically consider that a multinational defendant has resources to defend in the forum that the plaintiffs have selected.

Third, U.S. courts can express deference to the legal regimes of other countries by applying foreign law when that is appropriate—the choice-of-law issue. I reiterate, however, that the congressional purpose for using the phrase "law of nations" was to signal that conduct that might be tolerated in a foreign state might nonetheless be held to be a basis for liability in the courts of the United States. The U.S. courts would not be confronting the sovereign state of Nigeria about its legal rules; they would be saying that when a multinational corporation does business there, it may be held to the standards expected by the metropolitan country or countries where it is headquartered.

Fourth, under the law of nations as it has developed since Nuremberg, national courts have primary responsibility for addressing human rights violations. The obligations of temporary or permanent transnational courts are secondary. This principle has been elaborated in recent years, but it well antedates the ATCA. To be sure, a national court ought to make sure that its support for human rights in a distant land is not a hypocritical gesture that may mask unconcern about such rights closer to home.

A cogent example: in 1998, Abdoulaye Yerodia, the foreign minister of the Democratic Republic of the Congo, publicly urged citizens to kill opponents of the government who were mostly ethnic Tutsis. At that time, Belgian law asserted universal jurisdiction over genocide and crimes against humanity, and a Belgian court issued an arrest warrant for Yerodia. The DRC sued Belgium in the International Court of Justice in The Hague, claiming that under international law a serving foreign minister was immune from the criminal judicial jurisdiction of a foreign country. On February 14, 2002, the ICJ ruled in the DRC's favor and ordered the arrest warrant withdrawn. There was disagreement among the ICJ justices, three of whom dissented on the immunity question, and six on the question of remedy.

The question of hypocrisy was raised by Judge Bula-Bula, the DRC member of the tribunal. Judge Bula-Bula's opinion can be characterized as exclaiming: "What! Belgium is to give lessons on humanitarianism to the Congo?"

Where are the *Kiobel* plaintiffs to go for redress? Surely not back to the place where the killings, rapes, and plundering took place, to ask for a hearing from those responsible for the harm that was done. The U.S. has recognized, by granting them asylum, that return to their homeland is not an option. Are they then to wait for a decade or two or three until some transnational court is set up to address these issues? We know from recent examples that such courts might try the local offenders on criminal charges, but none of those courts has or exercises the power to hold the metropolitan country sponsors of terror accountable.

To repeat, Shell Oil is not a government. I have been to Shell's headquarters. They cannot be a government. They don't have a duty-free shop.

O TORTURED WORKERS, WON'T YOU MAKE ME A MERCEDES-BENZ

After the Second World War, Nazis fearing that their crimes would be exposed and punished fled Germany. Their escape routes were colloquially known as "ratlines." With the support of Catholic Church officials and Argentine politicians, Argentina was a preferred place of refuge. For example, Eichmann and Mengele were welcomed there.

In 1951, Mercedes-Benz built its first automobile manufacturing plant outside Germany—in the Buenos Aires suburb of González Catán.

Today, Mercedes-Benz has manufacturing and assembly facilities in thirty countries. The Mercedes website says:

"With offices in 93 locations worldwide and a corporate headquarters in Stuttgart, Germany, our global presence continues to grow." And: "Our vehicles are . . . distributed all over the world." [117]

From the early 1970s until the 1980s, the Argentine dictatorship's military and paramilitary forces carried on a campaign of murder, kidnapping, torture, repression, and disappearance of trade unionists, leftists, and others perceived as enemies of the state. The military junta bore the name Dictadura cívico-militar Argentina (Argentine Civil-Military Dictatorship), and colloquially Guerra Sucia (Dirty War).

Among the targets of this state-sponsored terror were union organizers and activists at the Mercedes plant. The United States government knew of the repressive violence fostered by the Argentine military junta, but it supported the junta unwaveringly. Declassified cable traffic shows that Henry Kissinger was a cheerleader for the Argentine leaders, encouraging and supporting the campaign of terror. The junta honored him. [118]

At the Mercedes-Benz plant, there was an unhappy confluence of these currents of history. In 2004, twenty-two Argentine residents filed suit in federal court in California. They sued the Mercedes parent corporation, DaimlerAG, alleging that DaimlerChrysler's Argentine subsidiary, MBA, "collaborated with state security forces to kidnap, detain, torture, and kill the plaintiffs and their relatives" during the Dirty War. [119] The plaintiffs served their complaint on MBUSA, the Mercedes U.S. manufacturer/distributor. The lawsuit alleged:

MBA sought to brutally punish plant workers whom MBA viewed as union agitators, and that MBA

collaborated with the Argentinian military and police forces in doing so. They also allege that MBA had
knowledge that the result of this collaboration would
be the kidnapping, torture, detention and murder of
those workers, and that the plan was implemented,
in part, in the following manner. First, MBA labeled
the appellants as "subversives" and "agitators" and
passed on this information to the state security forces. Second, MBA "had members of the military and
police forces stationed within" the González-Catán
plant. Third, MBA opened the plant to periodic raids
by those forces. Fourth, MBA hired Ruben Lavallen,
the police station chief who had been behind much
of the reign of terror and installed him as chief of security, providing legal representation to him when he
was "accused of human rights abuses." . . . Further . . .
MBA was pleased with the results of the raids and de-
tentions because those actions helped to end a strike,
restoring maximum production at the plant.[120]

Here was a lawsuit that evoked memories of Mercedes'
use of forced labor during the Second World War, and its
serendipitous establishment of a manufacturing plant in
Argentina, the country famed for sheltering Nazis.[121] Here
was yet another dictatorship operating with the encourage-
ment of the United States. Here were violations of fundamental human rights that directly benefitted a multinational
corporation with a worldwide footprint. Finally, here were
plaintiffs whose chance for redress in the courts of their own
country was, as the saying goes, "Slim, and none, and Slim
has left town."

Mercedes moved to dismiss the case, claiming that sub-
jecting them to a trial in California would violate due process

of law, specifically that the court did not have "personal juris-diction" over Mercedes with respect to these allegations. The United States Court of Appeals for the Ninth Circuit held that the court did have personal jurisdiction.

The Supreme Court granted certiorari. On January 14, 2014, the Court upheld Mercedes-Benz's position and ordered the case dismissed.[122] The first two paragraphs of Justice Ginsburg's opinion for the Court reveal just how for-malism can override and obscure reality:

> This case concerns the authority of a court in the United States to entertain a claim brought by foreign plaintiffs against a foreign defendant based on events occurring entirely outside the United States. The li-tigation commenced in 2004, when twenty-two Argentinian residents filed a complaint in the United States District Court for the Northern District of California against DaimlerChrysler Aktiengesellschaft (Daimler), a German public stock company, head-quartered in Stuttgart, that manufactures Mercedes-Benz vehicles in Germany. The complaint alleged that during Argentina's 1976–1983 "Dirty War," Daimler's Argentinian subsidiary, Mercedes-Benz Argentina (MB Argentina), collaborated with state security forces to kidnap, detain, torture, and kill certain MB Argentina workers, among them, plaintiffs or persons closely related to plaintiffs. Damages for the alleged human rights violations were sought from Daimler under the laws of the United States, California, and Argentina. Jurisdiction over the lawsuit was predicat-ed on the California contacts of Mercedes-Benz USA, LLC (MBUSA), a subsidiary of Daimler incorporated in Delaware with its principal place of business in New

Jersey. MBUSA distributes Daimler-manufactured vehicles to independent dealerships throughout the United States, including California.

The question presented is whether the Due Process Clause of the Fourteenth Amendment precludes the District Court from exercising jurisdiction over Daimler in this case, given the absence of any California connection to the atrocities, perpetrators, or victims described in the complaint. Plaintiffs invoked the court's general or all-purpose jurisdiction. California, they urge, is a place where Daimler may be sued on any and all claims against it, wherever in the world the claims may arise. For example, as plaintiffs' counsel affirmed, under the proffered jurisdictional theory, if a Daimler-manufactured vehicle overturned in Poland, injuring a Polish driver and passenger, the injured parties could maintain a design defect suit in California. . . . Exercises of personal jurisdiction so exorbitant, we hold, are barred by due process constraints on the assertion of adjudicatory authority.[123]

These paragraphs, like the judicial opinion they introduce, represent what one might call the "drone theory of judicial review," calling to mind that military drones arrive in the target zone at 50,000 feet of altitude, from which point it is impossible to see the humans on which death will soon be visited.

I put aside for the moment that Justice Ginsburg misrepresented what "plaintiffs' counsel" actually said in oral argument.[124] Also, Justice Ginsburg's "so exorbitant" statement is a classic "straw man" argument, for it presumes that if the Court allowed these plaintiffs to try their case, no future court would be able to see the difference between a run-of-the-mill car crash and years-long crimes of human rights committed by a multinational corporation with the connivance of the United States and a foreign government. The justice's formulation of what "this case concerns" and "the [only] question presented" scrubs the record clean of this concatenation of historical truths.

The Court discusses "specific personal jurisdiction," asking whether the lawsuit arises from Daimler's activity in California. It answers no. The Court then discussed "general personal jurisdiction," asking if Daimler's presence in California is so extensive that it may be sued there on any claim. Again, the answer is no. At that point, the analysis is done: plaintiffs are out of court.

The problem here is that the "specific" and "general" categories are the products of the Court's own invention. The Court devised them as convenient ways to analyze a question: Does the exercise of judicial power in a given case impose so great a burden on a litigant as to deny "due process"? In *Daimler*, the categories become self-imposed fetters. The Court is saying, "We are sorry that we cannot step out of this self-constructed mental prison; we have tied our shoelaces together."

In the nineteenth century, the Court had devised an equally confining personal jurisdiction test, imagining that trying cases with interstate features could pose insuperable issues of state sovereignty. This theory made it difficult to sue corporations doing business interstate. The 1877 expression of this theory, *Pennoyer v. Neff*,[125] was undermined in a series of decisions beginning in 1945 with *International Shoe Co. v. Washington*.[126] As the country emerged from the New Deal era, and the Second World War came to an end, the Court finally recognized that the modernization of transportation and communication, and the growth of interstate corporate commerce, required a more flexible view of due process and the practicality of litigation. At a more basic level, the Court recognized that people harmed by exercises of corporate power were entitled to reasonably practical access to justice. The Court explicitly overruled *Pennoyer* in 1977.[127]

One had hoped that the Court would escape from its self-created box of categories. In a 1982 decision, the Court said:

> The requirement that a court have personal jurisdiction flows . . . from the Due Process Clause. The personal jurisdiction requirement recognizes and protects an individual liberty interest. It represents a restriction on judicial power not as a matter of sovereignty, but as a matter of individual liberty. Thus, the test for personal jurisdiction requires that "the maintenance of the suit . . . not offend 'traditional notions of fair play and substantial justice.'"[128]

The *Daimler* opinion never gets to that Constitution-based question. Rather, it retreats into the very formalism that it claims to decry. The ghost of the deceased *Pennoyer* case sits crowned upon the grave thereof.[129]

Not surprisingly, there were dozens of amici curiae—friend of the court—briefs filed in the Supreme Court. Business-related groups predictably supported Daimler's position; human rights groups supported the plaintiffs. The Obama administration filed an amicus brief supporting Daimler.[130] The brief identified the "question presented" without regard to the harms suffered by the plaintiffs:

> Whether and under what circumstances the Due Process Clause of the Fourteenth Amendment per-

mits a court to exercise personal jurisdiction over a parent corporation based on its subsidiary's contacts with the forum State, in a case not arising out of, or related to either corporation's contacts with the State.

However, the government revealed its shameful moral obliquity in describing the "interest of the United States":

> The uncertain threat of litigation in United States courts, especially for conduct with no significant connection to the United States, could therefore discourage foreign commercial enterprises from establishing channels for the distribution of their goods and services in the United States, or otherwise making investments in the United States. Such activities are likely to be undertaken through domestic subsidiaries and thus are likely to implicate the decision below.

In short, if we allow United States courts to discuss torture and murder committed by a multinational with U.S. connivance, this might deter it and other multinationals from investing in the United States. It is worth noting in this context that multinationals, including Daimler, who gain a foothold in the United States have a dismal record with respect to workers' rights.[131]

The brief, taken as a whole, is as arid as a law school final examination. It does not once discuss the human rights issues at stake, only noting that the plaintiffs have alleged "torture" and that there is a law against that sort of thing. The brief does not acknowledge that the prohibition on torture is embodied in laws and international agreements with extraterritorial application, including the American Convention on Human Rights.

Let us imagine where the Court's analysis might have taken us, if it had viewed the Daimler litigation through the lens of history, as the Court did when deciding *International Shoe* in 1945. We can put the case in a context beginning in 1951, when Mercedes opened its Argentine plant, knowing that many who had taken up residence in Argentina were familiar with the Mercedes brand.

- After 1945, the international community defined, articulated, and enforced human rights. This process began in earnest with the establishment of the Nuremberg tribunal. It was given its most powerful impetus with the wave of decolonization and colonial liberation in the 1940s, 1950s, and 1960s. One major purpose of this movement for human rights was to define as unlawful and to remedy and prevent human rights violations in third world countries, carried out under the aegis of, and interest of, first world holders of state and monopoly power.
- One important principle in this body of law is that human rights violations are the concern of every state, and that states must provide an open forum to redress such violations. This principle must be tempered in ways that respect state sovereignty and that limit hypocritical assertions of power. However, when Mercedes decided to accept the benefits of state-sponsored terror, and to become complicit in it, the automobiles it produced in Argentina tainted an international web of commerce. The unlawful conduct furthered Mercedes' financial goals and the global political goals of the United States and its allies. Mercedes' decision to "go multinational" and to accept the benefits of international crime, can properly be seen as a waiver or forfeiture of any right to limit the forums where it may be sued.

- Since *International Shoe* was decided in 1945, the flow of people, goods, and information has become vastly more efficient. The costs of conducting litigation that concerns events distant from the forum state are a fraction of what they would have been back then.

- When a multinational such as Mercedes has a dispute with another multinational, or with a sovereign state, that dispute will often be heard in an international arbitral tribunal. The choice of which tribunal will not be limited by geographical boundaries—Paris, Stockholm, New York, Hong Kong, and so on.[132]

- If Mercedes got its wish, and the case were tried in Germany, German law would preclude the plaintiffs from recovering for the wrongs done to them. Thus, the argument about "personal jurisdiction" is really about whether there is any remedy at all. A thoughtful amicus brief filed in the case by the Center for Constitutional Rights makes this point.

- DaimlerAG does business all over the world. It has lawyers available to it in the United States. Its records are kept in ways that allow access via electronic means from any place in the world. The plaintiffs are shouldering much if not most of the cost of discovery that may take place in Argentina. Significant evidence has already been unearthed in U.S. State Department files. In the realm of transnational litigation, statutes, treaties, and special-purpose bilateral agreements make it as efficient to litigate such a case today as it was to litigate an interstate case fifty years ago.

- Many cases involving human rights violations have been and are being tried in forums distant from the events at issue—in The Hague before international tribunals and before various national courts.

- Corporate and governmental human rights violators have more power to wreak harm than any private actor. They act without regard to borders. They are recidivists. Far from being "exorbitant," the Daimler plaintiffs' theory identifies the true character of state and monopoly power. It is they, and not Justice Ginsburg, who live in the real world.

Notes

In these notes, Michael Tigar, *Law and the Rise of Capitalism*, 2nd ed. (New York: Monthly Review Press, 2000), is cited as "LRC2d." Articles by Michael E. Tigar are available at the Duke Law Library website, https://law.duke.edu/fac/tigar/bibliography/. *Monthly Review* articles can be found at http://monthlyreview.org/author/michaeletigar/. Unpublished legal cases cited as "WL" are available at the West Publishing's Westlaw site, which one can access in most law libraries. I have given many Wikipedia references because they are easily accessible. In these essays, I have borrowed ideas and words from some of my earlier works. Discussions of legal history draw upon LRC2d. My other books can be found on Amazon.com.

1. I discuss the colonial liberation movement and the imperial powers' response to it in Michael E. Tigar, *Thinking About Terrorism: The Threat to Civil Liberties in Times of National Emergency* (Chicago: American Bar Association, 2007).
2. Professors Brendan Nyhan and Jasom Reifler have published their research on the tendency of people to hold more strongly to beliefs in the face of contradictory evidence. See https://rationalwiki.org/wiki/Backfire_effect.
3. In the passage to which Marx refers, Moses is asking God for reassurance, and beseeches, "Show me thy glory." God replies, "No man shall see me, and live," but relents to the extent of telling Moses to stand on a rock, and "thou shalt

see my back parts, but my face shall not be seen." Exodus 33:23 (King James version).

4. The subtitle is from Vachel Lindsay's poem "Bryan, Bryan, Bryan, Bryan," in which Lindsay recalls the courage of Governor Altgeld, who pardoned the surviving Haymarket defendants.

5. See https://en.wikipedia.org/wiki/Haymarket_affair.

6. On Lucy Parsons, see Jacqueline Jones, *Goddess of Anarchy: The Life and Times of Lucy Parsons* (New York: Basic Books, 2018).

7. *Obergefell v. Hodges*, 576 U.S. —, 135 S.Ct. 2584 (2015), reversing *DeBoer v. Snyder*, 772 F.3d 388, 421 (6th Cir. 2014).

8. *Korematsu v. United States*, 323 U.S. 214 (1944) upheld the internment. Korematsu's and others' convictions for violating the internment order was vacated in *Korematsu v. United States*, 584 F.Supp. 1406 (N.D. Calif. 1984). The internment background and history is recounted in Jacobus tenBroek et al., *Prejudice, War and the Constitution* (Berkeley: University of California Press, 1970).. See also https://en.wikipedia.org/wiki/Korematsu_v._United_States.

9. See https://en.wikipedia.org/wiki/John_Henry_Faulk.

10. 163 U.S. 537 (1896).

11. See Jacobus tenBroek, *The Anti-Slavery Origins of the Fourteenth Amendment* (Berkeley: University of California Press, 1951).

12. 312 U.S. 496 (1941).

13. Frankfurter's Sacco-Vanzetti article is at http://www.theatlantic.com/magazine/archive/1927/03/the-case-of-sacco-and-vanzetti/306625/.

14. 319 U.S. 624 (1943).

15. 338 U.S. 49 (1949).

16. 95 U.S. 485 (1877).

17. 339 U.S. 629 (1950)

18. 1950 WL 78682

19. 1950 WL 78681.

20. See https://en.wikipedia.org/wiki/Charles_William_El-iot#Harvard_presidency.

21. Discussed in Michael E. Tigar, "Crisis in the Legal Profession: Don't Mourn, Organize," 37 *Ohio N. L. Rev.* 539, 547n37 (2011).

22. See https://www.theroot.com/idiot-teacher-asked-4th-grad-ers-to-give-3-good-reasons-1821982084.

23. Caroline Light, *Stand Your Ground: A History of America's Love Affair with Lethal Self-Defense* (Boston: Beacon Press, 2017).

24. Lorraine Boissenault, "What Will Happen to Stone Mountain, America's Largest Confederate Memorial?," https://www.smithsonianmag.com/history/what-will-hap-pen-stone-mountain-americas-largest-confederate-me-morial-180964588/.

25. On themes in this chapter see A. Smith and M. Freedman, eds., *How Can You Represent Those People?* (New York: Palgrave Macmillan, 2013). Some of the discussion in this section appeared in Michael Tigar, "Waiver of Constitutional Rights: Disquiet in the Citadel," 84 *Harv. L. Rev.* 1 (1970).

26. 397 U.S. 337 (1970).

27. See Angela J. Davis, *Arbitrary Justice* (Oxford: Oxford University Press, 2009); and Angela J. Davis, *Policing the Black Man: Arrest, Prosecution and Imprisonment* (New York: Pantheon, 2017).

28. 481 U.S. 279 (1987).

29. https://en.wikipedia.org/wiki/McCleskey_v._Kemp.

30. Sources for this essay are cited in Michael Tigar, "Lawyers, Jails and the Law's Fake Bargains," *Monthly Review* 53/3 (July–August 2001).

31. See https://www.aclu.org/news/gay-death-row-inmate-be-freed-texas.

32. A superb study of death penalty counsel is in Symposium, "Carter Center Symposium on the Death Penalty," 14 *Ga. St. U. L. Rev.* 329 (1998).

33. http://www.nytimes.com/2014/02/19/us/public-defend-
     ers-turn-to-lawmakers-to-try-to-ease-caseloads.html.

34. http://www.americanbar.org/content/dam/aba/events/le-
     gal_aid_indigent_defendants/2014/ls_sclaid_5c_the_mis-
     souri_project_report.authcheckdam.pdf.

35. California Commission on the Fair Administration of Jus-
     tice Final Report, June 30, 2008, http://digitalcommons.
     law.scu.edu/ncippubs/1.

36. 532 U.S. 182 (2001).

37. See *In re Humphrey*, 19 Cal.App.5th 1006 (2018)(funda-
     mental right to bail); *Ramos v. Sessions*, 2018 WL 905922
     (N.D. Calif. 2018)(bail in immigration proceedings).

38. *Murray v. Giarratano*, 492 U.S. 1 (1989) (no right to coun-
     sel once direct appeals have been completed). However,
     some statutory provisions provide for appointed counsel
     for capital defendants to challenge their convictions. Many
     law schools have Innocence Projects or Wrongful Convic-
     tion Clinics that provide pro bono assistance to incarcer-
     ated defendants.

39. 372 U.S. 335 (1963).

40. Nancy Gertner, "Having the Right to Appeal Is an Is-
     sue of Fairness," https://www.nytimes.com/roomforde-
     bate/2012/08/19/do-prosecutors-have-too-much-power/
     having-the-right-to-appeal-is-an-issue-of-fairness.

41. 397 U.S. 742 (1970). See Michael Tigar, "Waiver of Consti-
     tutional Rights: Disquiet in the Citadel," 84 *Harv. L. Rev.* 1
     (1970).

42. Citations to the case include 152 F.3d 381 (5th Cir. 1998)
     (direct appeal); 455 F.3d 508 (5th Cir. 2006). I was an
     expert witness on the ineffective assistance given by Mr.
     Hall's counsel, working with his lawyer Robert Owen.
     Many of the ideas in this discussion are based on Mr. Ow-
     en's and my collaboration, and I am indebted to him.

43. The phrase "reasoned moral response" originated in Jus-
     tice O'Connor's concurring opinion in *California v. Brown*,
     479 U.S. 538 (1987). See Linda E. Carter, Ellen S. Kreitz-

berg, and Scott W. Howe, *Understanding Capital Punishment Law*, 2nd ed. (New York: LEXISNEXIS, 2004).

44. For example, Supreme Court Justice Harry Blackmun sought for years to rationalize and demythologize death penalty law, before finally declaring that the task was impossible, and that he would "no longer tinker with the machinery of death," but would vote against imposition of the death penalty. *Callins v. Collins*, 510 U.S. 1141 (1984).

45. 466 U.S. 668, 687 (1984). See also *Hinton v. Alabama*, 134 S.Ct. 1081, 1083 (2014).

46. *Burdine v. Johnson*, 231 F.3d 950, vacated, 262 F.3d 336 (5th Cir. 2001), cert. denied, 536 U.S. 1120 (2003).

47. *Martinez-Macias v. Collins*, 979 F.2d 1067 (5th Cir, 1992).

48. 134 S.Ct. 1081 (2014).

49. See the discussion in Carter, Kreitzberg, and Howe, *Understanding Capital Punishment Law*, 218–19.

50. Michael E. Tigar, *Fighting Injustice* (Chicago: American Bar Association, 2002); Irving Stone, *Clarence Darrow for the Defense* (New York: Doubleday, 1941); Arthur Weinberg, ed., *Attorney for the Damned: Clarence Darrow in the Courtroom* (New York: Simon & Schuster, 1957), a collection of Darrow's courtoom speeches. In 2012, Santa Clara Law School held a reenactment of Darrow's trial for jury bribery. I was Darrow's "counsel." The video is at http://law.scu.edu/centennial/trial/.

51. For more detail about the case, see Barbara Bergman, "The Sweet Trials," in *Trial Stories,* ed. Michael Tigar and Angela Davis (St. Paul, MN: Foundation Press, 2008); and Kevin Boyle, *Arc of Justice* (New York: Henry Holt, 2004).

52. Richard Rothstein, *The Color of Law: A Forgotten History of How Our Government Segregated America* (New York: Liveright, 2017).

53. See *United States v. Bufalino*, 285 F.2d 60 (2d Cir. 1960): danger in conspiracy cases that jurors will "substitute a feeling of collective culpability for a finding of individual guilt." On the history and mythology of conspiracy, see Ti-

gar, "Essay: Crime-Talk, Rights-Talk and Doubletalk," 65 *Tex. L. Rev.* 101, 127–50 (1986); LRC2d, 82–95.

54. See Michael Tigar, *Thinking About Terrorism*, 128–30. 55. Albert Camus, *Lettres à un ami allemand* (Paris: Gallimard, 1948).

56. 307 U.S. 496 (1939).

57. 326 U.S. 501 (1946).

58. *Schwartz Torrance Investment Corp. v. Bakery & Confectionery Workers Union*, Local No. 31, 61 Cal.2d 766, 394 P.2d 921, 40 Cal.Rptr. 233 (1964), quoting from a concurring opinion of Justice William O. Douglas in one of the sit-in cases, *Lombard v. Louisiana*, 373 U.S. 267, 274 (1963). Justice Douglas said, in substance, that if you open a lunch counter, you should be considered to have agreed to give lunch to anybody who shows up, regardless of race.

59. *Amalgamated Food Employees Union Local 590 v. Logan Valley Plaza, Inc.*, 391 U.S. 308 (1968).

60. 407 U.S. 551 (1992).

61. 424 U.S. 507 (1976).

62. *Pruneyard Shopping Center v. Robins*, 447 U.S. 74 (1980).

63. *State v. Wicklund*, 589 N.W.2d 793 (Minn. Sup. Ct. 1999).

64. *Schneider v. New Jersey*, 308 U.S. 141, 145 (1939); see also *Martin v. City of Struthers*, 319 U.S. 141 (1943).

65. Material in this section draws on LRC2d, chapters 2, 13, 15, and 16.

66. LRC2d, 183–84.

67. Quoted in LRC2d, 184.

68. LRC2d, 191.

69. See LRC2d, chaps. 10–16. This process of displacing customary rights had been underway in Europe for centuries. Rulers of all description consolidated their authority by sponsoring codifications that purported to preserve and protect rights based on custom while in fact undermining them.

70. Sources for material in this section are in Tigar, "The Right of Property and the Law of Theft," 62 *Tex. L. Rev.* 1443 (1984).

71. The term SLAPP was coined by two law professors in the 1980s to describe a lawsuit designed to deter or punish speech about a public issue. See https://en.wikipedia.org/wiki/Strategic_lawsuit_against_public_participation.

72. In Canada, Native Americans are most often referred to as First Nation peoples.

73. 2017 WL 4618676 (N.D. Calif. 2017)(No. 17-cv-02824-JST).

74. Citing *Scheidler v. NOW, Inc.* 537 U.S. 393, 404 (2003).

75. *Red Lion Broadcasting Co. v. FCC*, 395 U.S. 367 (1969).

76. See https://en.wikipedia.org/wiki/FCC_fairness_doctrine.

77. See Edward S. Herman's work on monopoly control of mass communications, including Edward S. Herman and Noam Chomsky, *Manufacturing Consent: The Political Economy of the Mass Media* (New York: Pantheon Books,1988). Herman discussed the book's thesis and responded to criticism of his thesis in "The Propaganda Model Revisited," *Monthly Review* 69/8 (January 2018): 42. Herman's other work in *Monthly Review* can be found at https://monthlyreview.org/author/edwardsherman/. Robert W. McChesney's *Monthly Review* articles can be found at https://monthlyreview.org/author/robertwmcchesney/.

78. *Whitney v. California*, 274 U.S. 357, 377 (1927).

79. https://en.wikipedia.org/wiki/Citizens_United_v._FEC.

80. 558 U.S. 310 (2010).

81. Quoted in Michael Tigar, "It Does the Crime but Not the Time: Corporate Criminal Liability in Federal Law," 17 *Am. J. Crim. Law* 211 (1990).

82. *New York Central Railroad v. United States*, 212 U.S. 481, 492–93 (1909).

83. See https://en.wikipedia.org/wiki/Daniel_Ellsberg.

84. See *Gravel v. United States*, 408 U.S. 606 (1972).

85. *Federalist* No. 45. The Federalist Papers are available on line at, e.g., http://files.libertyfund.org/files/788/0084_LFeBk.pdf.

86. 17 U.S. Code § 105 (1982).

87. Hans Magnus Enzensberger, *Politics and Crime* (New York: Seabury Press, 1974), 13.

88. See Tigar, "The Right of Property and the Law of Theft."

89. RICO, the Racketeer-Influenced and Corrupt Organizations Act, 18 U.S.C. 1961–68, provides enhanced criminal punishments for those who commit a "pattern" of acts consisting of certain offenses. The statute provides for a civil remedy for victims of such conduct, and provides for treble damages, attorney fees, and nationwide service of process. See https://en.wikipedia.org/wiki/Racketeer_Influenced_and_Corrupt_Organizations_Act.

90. Complaint, *Smithfield Foods, Inc. v. UFCW*, No. 3:07CV641, 2008 WL 1825139 (E.D.Va. 2008).

91. See Wayne LaFave, *Criminal Law*, 4th ed. (St. Paul, MN: West Publishing, 2003), 1012–16.

92. Karl Renner, "The Institutions of Private Law and Their Social Functions," quoted and discussed in LRC2d, 268–69.

93. *R. v. Journeymen-Taylors of Cambridge*, 88 Eng. Rep. 9 (1721).

94. See Wythe Holt, "Labour Conspiracy Cases in the United States, 1805–1842: Bias and Legitimation in Common Law Adjudication," 22 *Osgoode Hall L. J.* 591 (1984). David Paul Brown's jury speech is in *Forensic Speeches of David Paul Brown* (Philadelphia: King & Baird, 1873), 104.

95. On the origins of "conspiracy," see Tigar, "Crime-Talk, Rights-Talk and Doubletalk," in LRC2d. It is interesting to note that the early bourgeois rebels often joined themselves with an oath of mutual assistance.

96. Darrow, *Industrial Conspiracies* (Portland: Turner, Newman & Knispel 1912), 4–5.

97. 158 U.S. 564 (1895).

98. http://www.damfirm.com/human-cost-construction/Four; https://www.dol.gov/dol/aboutdol/history/mono-reg-safepart05.htm.

99. *Brotherhood of Railway Trainmen v. Virginia ex rel*, Virginia State Bar, 377 U.S. 1 (1964).

100. See *Tiller v. Atlantic Coast Line Railroad Co.*, 318 U.S. 54 (1943), discussing history of injured-worker rights.

101. Comment, "The Creation of a Common Law Rule: The Fellow Servant Rule 1837–1860," 132 *U. Penn. L. Rev.* 579 (1984), http://scholarship.law.upenn.edu/cgi/viewcontent.cgi?article=4623&context=penn_law_review.

102. *Cintas Corp. v. Unite Here*, 601 F.Supp.2d 571 (S.D.N.Y.), aff'd, 355 Fed.Appx. 508 (2d Cir. 2009).

103. https://en.wikipedia.org/wiki/Prem_Reddy.

104. http://www.latimes.com/business/la-fi-prime-healthcare-sexual-harassment-20151024-story.html; https://www.dailynews.com/2017/03/13/medical-board-of-california-chief-faces-question-after-sexual-misconduct-vote/; http://www.sfgate.com/bayarea/article/Prime-Healthcare-reportedly-subject-of-FBI-probe-2399751.php; https://www.eastbaytimes.com/2007/07/12/high-profit-hospital-chain-built-at-patients-expense-2/.

105. *Prime Healthcare Services., Inc. v. SEIU*, 2013 WL 3873074, 2013 WL 6500069 (S.D. Calif. 2013), aff'd, 642 Fed.Appx. 665 (9th Cir.), cert. denied, 136 S.Ct. 2532 (2016).

106. *Prime Healthcare Services., Inc. v. SEIU*, 147 F.Supp.3d 1094 (S.D. Calif. 2015), appeal dismissed, No. 15-56965, 8/22/17 (9th. Cir.).

107. 569 U.S. 108 (2013).

108. *United States v. Guest*, 383 U.S. 745 (1966), interpreting Ku Klux Klan act to permit prosecution of those assisting local police in the murder of civil rights workers.

109. See http://www.scotusblog.com/2017/07/introduction-alien-tort-statute-corporate–liability-plain-english/.

110. *The Paquete Habana*, 175 U.S. 677 (1900).

111. David Vine, *Base Nation: How U.S. Military Bases Abroad Harm America and the World* (New York: Metropolitan Books, 2015); David Vine, "'We're Profiteers'": How Military Contractors Reap Bilions from U.S. Military Bases Overseas," *Monthly Review* 66/3 (July-August 2014): 82.

112. See https://en.wikipedia.org/wiki/Nicaragua_v._United_States.

113. See LRC2d, 291–319.

114. See Tigar, "It Does the Crime but Not the Time."

115. See John C. Balzano, "Direct Effect Jurisdiction Under the Foreign Sovereign Immunities Act: Searching for an Integrated Approach," 24 *Duke J. of Comp. & Int. L.* 2 (2013).

116. When Spain sought to extradite Augusto Pinochet for trial on charges of torture and genocide, his admitted claim to immunity as former president of Chile did not reach far enough to insulate him from liability for those crimes. See http://en.wikipedia.org/wiki/Augusto_Pinochet. In the *Yerodia* case, the International Court of Justice spoke cautiously about the immunity doctrine and its reach. You can read about the case at http://en.wikipedia.org/wiki/Abdoulaye_Yerodia_Ndombasi.

117. See https://www.mbusa.com/en/about-us; see also https://en.wikipedia.org/wiki/Mercedes-Benz. From 1926 to 1988, the parent corporation was Daimler-Benz AG; from 1998 to 2007, the parent was DaimlerChrysler AG; from 2007 to the present, Daimler AG. At all times, corporate headquarters was in Stuttgart, Germany, https://en.wikipedia.org/wiki/Daimler_AG.

118. Declassified cables showing Kissinger's complicity are available at nsarchive2.gwu.edu.

119. 644 F.3d 909, 912 (9th Cir. 2011).

120. 644 F.3d at 912.

121. See https://en.wikipedia.org/wiki/Ratlines, WorldWar II aftermath.

122. *Daimler AG v. Bauman*, 571 U.S. 117 (2014).

123. 571 U.S. at 120.

124. https://www.supremecourt.gov/oral_arguments/argument_transcripts/2013/11-965_g2hk.pdf, also at 2013 WL 5845699. Plaintiffs' counsel, under close questioning by the justices, was saying no more than (a) there might be a set of facts on which to base personal jurisdiction in such

a case, even though a U.S. court might find it inconvenient to exercise that power; and (b) such a result would be permissible because Daimler's counsel had failed to brief the issue properly. I have argued hundreds of cases, and seven of those in the Supreme Court. I think most advocates would agree that it is unfair to latch on to an imperfectly expressed thought and use it to hammer the client.

125. 95 U.S. 714 (1877).

126. *International Shoe Co. v. Washington*, 326 U.S. 310 (1945).

127. *Shaffer v. Heitner*, 433 U.S. 186 (1977).

128. *Insurance Company of Ireland v. Compaignie des Bauxites de Guinee*, 456 U.S. 694 (1982).

129. A paraphrase of Thomas Hobbes: "The Papacy is not other than the Ghost of the deceased Roman Empire, sitting crowned upon the grave thereof."

130. 2013 WL 3377321.

131. See https://www.nytimes.com/2015/09/25/business/workers-at-alabama-truck-parts-factory-vote-to-join-uaw.html. Hourly wages of workers who build Mercedes vehicles in the United States are less than half of those paid to workers at the Mercedes plants in Germany.

132. See M. Ostrove, C. Salomon, and B. Shifman, eds., *Choice of Venue in International Arbitration* (Oxford: Oxford University Press, 2014).

Index